Blade in the Shadow

a memoir

Jillian Halket

Guts Publishing

Published in London by Guts Publishing 2021

Cover art © 1912 Alexej von Jawlensky
Cover design © 2021 Julianne Ingles

ISBN
978-1-8384719-2-7 (paperback)
978-1-8384719-3-4 (ebook)

Printed in the UK

www.gutspublishing.com

For Stuart – we were always three.

Praise for *Blade in the Shadow*

"A dark, rich account of how it feels to live with OCD, glimmering with light and hope. A testament to the power of naming what you are and a wrenching portrayal of the mind in all of its colours. A bold pursuit of a life that is more than just a way to survive."
— Jessica Andrews, author of *Saltwater* (Portico Prize 2020)

"A difficult, inspiring story, told with raw honesty and immense courage. We need more voices like Jillian Halket's in conversations around mental health in Scotland."
— Elsa Maishman, *The Scotsman*

"*Blade in the Shadow* is a raw and gripping account of the unseen pain and terror that can be part of life with OCD. This book is vivid, lyrical and at times startlingly honest and is a valuable opportunity to access the lived experience of someone with a form of OCD that causes violent, intrusive thoughts. The writing is fresh, frank and fearless and I highly recommend it."
— Catherine Simpson, author of *TrueStory* and *When I Had a Little Sister*

"A dark but hauntingly beautiful memoir that will bring comfort to anyone living with OCD as a reminder that you're not alone. Jillian's writing is gorgeous, it will tear you apart before putting you back together again. This is exactly the kind of book I've come to expect from Guts Publishing – raw and unflinchingly honest yet determinedly hopeful."
— Sarah McLean, *Scot Lit Blog*

Blade in the Shadow

Knives

Every night I die.

The ephemeral hours of night break and dawn bleeds in. The dream slows – the fabric of one strange reality unthreading, desperately trying to stitch itself to another. My fingers trace the line of my skull and pause at the hollows of my eyes. I move my hands over my cotton underwear and feel the curve of my body.

I'm still here.

The sweet relief soon turns saccharine and my back teeth ache as I try to imagine making it through another day like this. Another night like this. Oblivion would be sweeter still than these dreams of ragged flesh.

There is a certain way things need to be done. A perverted set of rituals. I crawl to the edge of my bed and climb carefully over the side. If I were to stand up near the end I would trip and the bedpost would drive up into my vagina and rip me from the inside. The image of my impaled body rotting on the bedpost burns in my vision. A sad grey sack.

The room is airless and my mouth has an alloy tang like my spit is made from metal. Adrenaline tears through every fibrous nerve of my body. Just like every other morning I reach for the door handle and find I cannot open it. I hit my head off the frame again and again and pray for it to split open and let the worms and grubs pour out. The burrowing obsessions have rotted my brain and left porous holes behind like old cauliflower.

In a viral loop in my mind the same four words repeat: *I am not safe.*

Defeat stills my body and I drag myself back into bed. Careful to climb over the side not the edge. Once buried I pull the blanket over my head in a kind of futile sanctuary. From a formless dark shape – the obsession has latched on.

I am not safe.

It will happen today.

There is no escape, no place to hide and nothing to do to stem the coming tide. Like the doctor told me I breathe deeply – in for four, hold for four, out for four – and with razor thin desperation I try to convince myself that I'm okay and that nothing bad can happen to me here.

This is a lie.

Red.

There is a single shift, atomic in size, and then the violence tears through my mind. My eyes are ripped from my skull. Blood jets down my cheek as the stalk of my eye is severed. The pulp like rotted fruit. Everything goes black. Howling like a desperate animal before slaughter, I claw at my face. The metallic salt of my blood singes my nostrils. In my arms I cradle my skull, trying to hold the plated bone together.

Please make it stop.

I rock back and forth and wait for the end to come.

Hours pass and I awaken drenched in a slick sweat of confusion. My hands search my face, pass over my underwear and I find I'm still here.

2

And the ritual repeats.

There is no comfort in this kind of familiarity. It is endless. A purgatory made of blood and spit and bone. But rituals must be observed and so I climb over the side of my bed. If I stood up near the end I would trip and the bedpost would rip me in two.

Seven.

Seven times seven.

Forty-nine is better.

As I touch everything made of wood in the bedroom forty-nine times the dull static of the television in the background keeps me company. There is a close-up of a girl with brilliant blue eyes. Little shards of glass.

Red.

Ommetaphobia is the fear of eyes.

It is surprisingly difficult to avoid eye gore. Directors in films use it as a shorthand. They know it's one of the most vulnerable places on the human body. They know showing a character being hurt there will elicit the kind of response they desire. A trigger. But I still don't avoid films or television shows. One, films provide me with some kind of method to understand this world, and two, their violence feels zany, often bordering on the absurd. I can't explain but sometimes the colour palette just looks off or the effects are a bit laughable. A googly eye hanging off deck.

My own obsessions however, cut clean through the bone.

It will be three more years before I know anything real about obsessions and compulsions and the disorder that binds them. The three small initials that will come to dictate so much of my life.

I spy my reflection in the darkened bloom of the television set. A ghoul, eyes dense as osmium. These days there is no point in trying to make myself look presentable. Even through a sickly

3

layer of make-up the shadows are still there. My skin is dirt pale and filmy like spoilt milk and deep gashes mark the sides of my lips from biting them in the night. I like to chew the little pieces of skin. To tear the rags of flesh off when I know I shouldn't.

If I try to smile the wounds split further.

In my bedroom I open the dusty curtains. I swear I've been trying to get in the habit of opening them but some days the light is so oppressive it's as if my feelers are being burned off by a cruel child with a magnifying glass.

The town is faded. Rows of council houses with a small pub and an abandoned community centre. I hide behind the curtain when I see a group of people walking past though it's not like they ever see me anyway. I'm the Notre Dame bell ringer of this small Scottish town. The same copper hair as Quasi and the same hunger to be around people and not be seen as a monster.

I lift my eyes to the miserable sky. From the grey furrows of clouds I can half make out a new light. If I squint I think there might be a waning star burning just beyond the horizon. This is almost worse, this small and beautiful thing, and I wonder if it might be easier to blight all feeling. At least then I'd be free of this madness. The star falls behind the clouds but I know it's still there and so I suppose I have no choice but to stay.

At least for a little while longer.

Time does not move in a linear, predetermined way. Not these days. I find myself stuck between planes of time like glass, trapped between moments until they fracture and I'm propelled into a new space. Time shifts in such a way and when I come to I'm in a car with my sister Lydia.

"Alright, my pea?" she says and kisses my forehead. At her affection I turn upwards like a desperate flower to an unfathomable sun. The warmth doesn't go all the way through to my bones though and soon the edges of my vision are

4

obscured by a dark vignette. Though I try to follow the bright story she's telling me, Lydia's words begin to bend backwards and she slips out of focus.

Fighting to hold myself in the present moment, I fasten my attention on her face and notice there are dashes of freckles across the bridge of her nose like little people travelling from one side to the other. My sister is beautiful. When she smiles she lights up from within as if spun from pure sunlight. There is a strange aching in this moment, a longing to shrink from my own skin and step into hers, to see the world as she does. The distance between us, arising from the hold the obsessions have wrought on my life, makes me sad. The love that ties us is as strong as it's ever been, but this sickness holds me hostage.

I am not nearly the person I once was.

The cars on the motorway push close to us and my grip on my seatbelt tightens. The panic splinters in my chest and I twist in my seat as if I'm a nervous bee bouncing off the window trying to get out. I try to focus on Lydia's story but her words are becoming more and more alien.

Red.

Lydia is thrown into the dashboard. In the crack of a second her beautiful head splits and her once bright eyes dull. Her limbs stick out at a weird, crooked angle like a puppet stuffed into a toy box backwards. Her light dims and everything is lost to me. I close my eyes.

Come back.

This isn't real.

The hum of Lydia's steady talk brings me back. Her eyes are fixed upon me like beacons. "Are you okay?"

I nod. "I'm fine."

We pull up to the cottage where Mama and my stepdad Jim live (full name James Brown, not unlike the singer and blessed with the kind of good nature that allows this joke to be made

5

countless times). There is a deep glow to the land here, the light scattering in golden contours confusing the line between the material and immaterial. It is fable-like in its beauty, the fields and heather full of unnamed colours. Mama's hearing aids screech with feedback as she holds me and on the couch we all sit close as sardines bundled under the same blanket. My family talk and I try to hold onto them. Hold onto myself. My family speak quietly and share biscuits and their lovely warmth almost breaks through. In the moon tides they are my lighthouse keepers. I just need to find my way to them.

In the kitchen I make tea and notice a tear in the floral wallpaper. The strain of the kettle's whistle startles me and I knock a cup over. It must be a few minutes that I stare at the jagged pieces on the floor. As I go to scoop them up it's difficult to resist pressing my hands and wrists deep into the glass.

Red.

Mama is quick to make her way to me but I'm already hysterical. I pull at the wool of her cardigan and try desperately to stop myself from sticking the shards of glass into my skin. She clutches me and mumbles into my hair, "You're safe." Lydia puts her hand on my shoulder with sorrow held thinly on her face. I sit folded in on myself, reticent, and Mama cups my hands in hers and tells me, with a steadfast certainty that could hold the very planets themselves together, that while I can't, she'll hold onto hope for me.

We drive back to the bleak flat. Lydia asks me if I'm okay and I tell her she doesn't need to worry. Truthfully, I'm tired of being a burden to them. After a radioactive microwave dinner I climb the stairs to bed. A shattering noise wakes me in the night and I scurry over the side of the bed – not the end. My rituals are so embedded that not even a real and present threat makes a difference.

6

The noise is coming from next door and in my paranoid state I think it must be the neighbours trying to break in, so I run down to the front door and check the locks. There are drunken people screaming and shambling outside in the landing and I become convinced they can see my shadow underneath the door.

I am not safe.

The sickly humidity presses close and I go to the kitchen and pick the largest of the knives. The leather of the couch sticks to my back as I stare straight ahead into the darkness, the silver of the knife glinting as the headlamps of cars pass by. It grows quiet and my heart begins to slow and I curl up on the couch hoping for the sweet respite of sleep. I'm careful to keep the knife beside me – just in case. My eyes close for a second before the silent fathoms rise and click back open again like a broken doll.

Red.

I could stab myself in my sleep with the knife.

From safeguard to enemy the knife turns on me and I wearily hide it in the back of the drawer.

Red.

I could sleepwalk to the kitchen, get the knife and stab myself in my sleep.

And that is all it takes.

The virulence of the thought takes me hostage. In coarse whispers I try to convince myself, "Don't stab, don't stab, don't stab. It's okay. You'll be alright." But the endless repetition only serves to strengthen the obsession.

Stab.

My mind has locked onto that single word and it doesn't understand the difference between do and don't. I crawl into bed. Over the side not the edge. I prop myself against the wall and make sure to keep moving my toes. I have to stay awake so

I don't end up hurting myself. The phantom of the knife has followed me and though the room is dark, I'm not alone. My vision sweeps in and out of focus and from vermilion droplets of blood, dark moths take shape. There, lurking in the corner, they spread their wings and wait.

I stay up all night until dawn bleeds in.

Blackwood

I didn't know I had obsessive compulsive disorder until I was twenty-one years old.

Four years before in a small village called Blackwood, I lay in the summer starched grass like a fallow deer. The bonfire spat in the background, coating the air in amber.

"Another drink?"

Through the grass I crawled to the fireside, my hands careful of the tiny bugs that shivered in the moss underneath me. Near the edge I found my bottle with its nectar flourishing in the flame light. Emily nestled in beside me. Her blonde hair was spiked up in tufts, little golden peaks against the fathomless depths behind her. We toasted our bottles of wine and I smiled at her bright, beautiful head.

Red.

I closed my eyes. I couldn't look at my friend without seeing her skin torn away from her jaw, the pearls of her teeth exposed and her tongue limp like a slug.

At seventeen I knew almost nothing of obsessive compulsive disorder and anything I did know was related to contamination obsessions and hand-washing compulsions. There was no way for me to reconcile the violence in my mind as the same thing.

Turning away from the gore of Emily's new face, I dug my fingers into my arm to distract me. A pink blossom formed. I was more than this. More than these thoughts. Sometimes it was just hard to remember that I was hemmed in by this body and its blood.

Around the bonfire my friends drifted like satellites. Some chased each other around the woods and howled into the inky sky like wolves. Most of them had started drinking when they were young. In Scotland it's not uncommon for people to start drinking in their early teens, sometimes even younger.

At seventeen I was a late bloomer.

It had never interested me much before. Until that first drink I had no idea what it could do for me. After that first drink my devotion was fervid. Holy, almost. I came to view alcohol as a kind of antidote to all my anxieties. It allowed me to shed my tired insecurities and for once I felt right, as though this is how I should have always been. The alcohol brought weight and shape to my being and for once I was steadfast and sure of myself.

There was something more.

My friends howled like wolves and I finished my wine, lying down beside the fire to watch the flame salamanders' dance. It took everything not to plunge my hands into the flames.

In truth, the confidence and excitement of alcohol was only superficial; secondary to the essential state I was really seeking.

The quietening of my mind.

If there was a time before the violent thoughts, I can't remember it so it might as well not exist. I don't know what it was like before my brain showed me the people I loved with

10

their faces cut open or skin flayed off from burns. A time where I didn't have to pass my hands over my body in the morning to make sure my flesh hadn't been torn in the night.

From a young age I tried to stop the obsessive thoughts with rituals. I now know the correct name for them – compulsions. At first the rituals were physical compulsions. When I was doing the dishes I would stack the cutlery neatly to keep Mama (big spoon), Lydia (little spoon) and Dad (fork) all safe. In my bedroom I scribbled their names on pieces on paper and floated them in a drawer filled with water. That was of course until the stench from the mouldering water was discovered by my very confused Mama. I followed along with all the common superstitions, magpies and cracks and broken backs, but my own were better. They had more chance of protecting us.

As I grew older the rituals turned from outwardly physical ones into internal ones.

If I had a bad thought, I would balance it with a good one. When a violent image would burrow into my brain, I would picture something bright and happy after it. To stop Mama dying I would count to seven while walking carefully on the floor tiles on the kitchen. Until of course I realised that seven times seven would be a better, safer, more powerful choice and forty-nine became my number.

In bed I'd lie awake as thoughts of people dying in grisly freak accidents burned in my vision. What horrified me most is that sometimes a pained shriek of laughter would escape from me when these images appeared. I would punish myself for laughing, for being bad. I developed a ritual for that too. Hitting my head against the wall repeatedly.

As I grew older the rituals became embedded in my everyday life. After a while I didn't have to force myself to imagine a happy thought after a bad one – it just happened automatically. My brain was constantly equalising and creating a safe and stable loop to protect me and my family from being hurt. By the time I reached high school the process was automatic and there were no more borders between my rituals and waking life itself. Still, the thoughts continued and I grew weary of their acidic intensity.

Red.

In Chemistry class the sharp smell from the Bunsen burner inflamed my nostrils and my mind strickened. *I'm burning.* In panic I clawed at my face to make sure I was still there. The obsessions were virulent by nature, infecting every part of me.

But most importantly, they were phantoms.

The unrelenting obsessions, the perpetual anxiety and the strange warping of reality – they were the truly destructive thing. The obsessions of violence could in truth be centred on anything. Years later I read an article about a man who had a crippling phobia of buttons and another who feared the number thirteen. My obsessions just so happened to focus on violence instead and yet it shamed me to be so terrified of a vague, shapeless threat.

I was careful never to mention the violent thoughts to anyone for fear that I would upset someone who had a lived experience of such a thing. What frightened me most was the threat that never fully realised, the blade in the shadow.

I lived in a world that constantly felt on the edge of chaos. All I wanted was to feel safe.

Safe.

The most important thing in the world to me.

There is a genetic component to obsessive compulsive disorder, and there is also an environmental one. The two go hand in hand. The gene can be latent until some environmental trauma triggers it. There is a dark shape, a formless word in the back of my mind that I haven't been able to verbalise for years.

Dad.

My dad was an angry man. He'd grit his teeth, break things and kick walls. One time he even broke his toe in a bout of instant karma which was actually quite funny – in a way. There was the time he handed Lydia a knife and told her, "Go on. Stab me," while I watched from behind the couch crying for them to stop.

Dad left us alone a lot as kids. The night Mama took off her wedding ring he had left us hungry at home while he was out at the pub drinking and gambling and she was at work. The most insidious times were when he was in the room but you felt entirely alone. He didn't acknowledge my sister or me. He didn't ask us questions or pay attention to anything we said – school projects were given an apathetic nod or a spelling mistake would be called to our attention before his eyes glazed over and found the television screen again. Before bed we'd call out in a reedy wail, "Love you, Dad." He didn't say he loved us back. With no one to see you, you shrink until you become smaller and smaller and take up less and less space. He neglected us and like seedlings we desperately tried to take root in what little soil he gave us.

With Mama we flourished. She painted us back in with bold brush strokes and brilliant colours; telling us how loved and special we were. She kept us safe and protected us from most of his anger. She tried to contain it but like radiation it leaked through the whole house.

Though anxious and lonely as a child, I still had happy times. My beautiful hippy mother brought out the magick in the world for me. I was a pagan child caught between countryside and concrete; raised in teepees in Braemar in the summer and the Taywood estate the rest of the year.

I lived in a house split between chaos and beauty. A broken father and a mum who weaved her golden light into us like

Kintsugi. We were dirty heathens. Shamanic practice was our way of life. I'd absent-mindedly brush past poppets (tiny figures of people used for witchcraft) when looking for an ice lolly on a particularly hot day. The village priest eyed the animal bones on the walls when he came to enquire why I wasn't at Sunday mass. Mama spoke of life in the major and minor arcana of the Tarot and we came to see life in patterns and symbols. In my room I ate Kit Kats and watched reality television while downstairs hedge fund managers were tied up in sleeping bags and drummed into astral projection. The neighbourhood curtain-twitchers saw the Audis of businessmen and lawyers parked on the street and assumed my mama was a sex worker. I just laughed. My hair smelt of sage and sweetgrass and I wore sandals in the snow.

The divorce was one of the best things to happen to our family even if I couldn't see it at the time. Though he was unpredictable and made me nervous I still loved my dad. He'd often whisper that he and I were the same, that we had some kind of bond that Mama and Lydia couldn't understand. He made me feel guilty for ever thinking badly of him. I came to pity him and feared he would be lonely without us and so chose to stay with him on weekends where most of the time he'd fall asleep with a beer, or worse, I'd be left in the flat alone. But he always had an explanation, easy words that made you feel off and a bit sick but you accepted them anyway because you wanted him to love you. It wouldn't be till years later that I would manage to unhook some of his talons and fight back against his narcissistic abuse.

After the divorce Mama was at least physically free and she started to build a life for us three girls. We were happy like that. A few years later I was gifted a stepdad who taught me that blood of the covenant is thicker than water of the womb.

And one of the things Mama feared most, what she promised us would never happen, happened – we lost the house. Frantic with worry at trying to pay off the bailiffs and heavies from Dad's gambling debts and now desperate to find a new house, Mama remained steadfast for us girls. One night as she and Jim were driving home from their pagan shop in Strathaven they happened upon a small village. Life is full of small turns of fate like that – ones that look catastrophic on the surface but are actually a blessing.

I am grateful that we lost that house because without it I would have never had Blackwood. A small village in South Lanarkshire with barely more than a few thousand people. A hearth where I made friends and found what little footing I could without knowledge of my disorder.

In the woods the fire salamanders finished their dance. The alcohol had blunted the colours and depth of the world. The violent thoughts faded and I was left numb. The world was quiet. The fire burned low and I said goodbye to my friends and walked home. The forest was subsumed by strange starlight and amethyst wildflowers bloomed in the shade. Amongst the gnarled limbs of the trees I larked around pretending to be a wild cat.

At 4am I returned home having forgotten my key again. Scratches from errant bushes lined my legs and my shoes were soggy from the walk back but I'd come too early to wake Mama or Jim so I passed out in the shed, the beetles making beds in my fanned out hair and my fingers turning purple with the cold.

My mind was quiet.

Girls and Boys

I didn't have to come out.

Everyone already knew.

When I was younger I'd lay down on the damp blue bath mat and close my eyes. When I touched myself I thought of both the men and women I saw on 90s television. Clark Kent and Lois Lane. Line by line, pixel by pixel, I printed out pictures of nude women on our tiny dodgy printer but then got so worried my family would find them that I hid them in the hollow of my acoustic guitar. As a child I drew a muscle man on my pillow under the case and kissed him goodnight. I have to laugh now imagining what Mama must have thought as she did housework and found muscle man and the naked ladies in my guitar.

As a child I wore peach dungarees stained green at the knees from grass and floated around the house in an alien mask with a voice changer. This unnerved Lydia. When I hit puberty, I became self-conscious of my soft body and wore a swimsuit under all my clothes. When I was a little older, I bought the strongest sports bra I could find to flatten my chest.

I had always been a lonely child and the secret of my obsessions did little but distance me from others. I sought connection in different ways. I had a wonderful family and so I spent a lot of time with them. I devoured books and films and as a teen I found solace in online forums discussing them with others who were just as introverted and anxious. At this time the Internet was a different place. Real names weren't exchanged on the forums and instead you chose a username and avatar. I grew close to a girl called Megan and we switched information and went on to spend Friday nights together talking on webcam. She lived in Surrey and was a couple of years older than me. I dreamed of one day getting the bus down and finally meeting her in person. But it never happened.

It's strange how much that relationship meant to me though, for one so brief. It made me more myself. Megan accepted me. I never had to explain myself – she just understood. I felt comfortable around her. Around fifteen I came across a Tumblr page with different rainbow flags on it. With a ravenous fervour I read through the descriptions like a pirate stumbling across a chest of treasured gold.

This was it.

The pink, blue and yellow flag.

Pan.

Like the creature of folklore.

Wooded glens and dark fruit.

Attraction.

Regardless of sex.

Of gender.

Yes.

That's me. I thought.

I ordered a pansexual necklace online and wore it under the shirt of my school uniform. I didn't tell my family or friends but

I could tell they knew. I was privileged enough to be able to exist without explaining – a kind of privilege denied to so many.

Understanding my sexuality was one thing but I was years away from understanding my OCD. The thoughts were always a part of me. The world would shift and I would no longer be able tell a vulture from a dove. My unyielding belief was: *Something bad is going to happen and I cannot do anything to stop it.*

The first years of high school were difficult. Often in the middle of class or even just before the school day ended, I reached a breaking point where I could no longer function. I had sensory issues. The fluorescent lights hurt my head and I couldn't bear the constant noise of people shrieking and shoving past me in the corridor. I had trouble seeing past the images in my mind to the worksheets in front of me. A teacher would be flagged down by my kind classmates and they'd ask if I was alright. Their gentle hand on my shoulder would make me feel sick. I knew they were only trying to help but I wished they wouldn't touch me. The school office knew me well. They popped me in the side room and made the all too familiar call home. Mama worked desperate hours to support the family and never stopped for a moment. I remember the guilt burning in my chest. Why can't I just hold on a bit longer? I thought.

But Mama always blazed in like a marvel. Her serious eyes searched for me before scooping me into her arms like a fierce mama bear protecting her cub. She would absentmindedly nod at reception but her attention never left me. She hugged me and I burrowed in. My Mama. Her lovely perfume and her warm, freckled skin. She never mentioned me disturbing her, or the money she had lost that day by coming to get me. She just told me everything was going to be okay.

"We're going home now."

At seventeen, the mornings would begin the same way. I'd wake – my nerves already flayed and my mind itching with static noise. Mama was concerned that I was throwing up almost every morning and had a permanently upset stomach. She took me to the doctor who after a quick examination couldn't find any physical reason for my sickness. I felt like a fraud. If there had been another doctor that day I wonder if things might have been different. Would they have seen the signs? Would I have been honest about the things I saw in my mind? I'm not sure. The doctor prescribed sea sickness tablets and waved me out of his office. I took my tablets and forced myself onto the bus every morning and by my final year I managed more days than not.

My days in high school ended quietly. After four rejections I was conditionally accepted into Glasgow University. I met my grade requirements and applied for the various grants and loans that would allow me to pursue higher education. On the night of my acceptance, I woke Mama and Lydia to tell them. We cried and did an odd victory dance in the darkened corridor and though I tried to sleep when dawn came I was still awake – one eye fixed on the Glasgow University online brochure – dreaming of a future where I was a little less sad.

A little less mad.

I turned eighteen and spent my days with my friends in the sunlit woodland, building bonfires and drinking. All of us were on different paths, each divining a different kind of future for ourselves but for now we had one last chance to be together, just as we were.

Quietly pan, I'd had crushes on boys and girls and even thought I had fallen in love with a boy. I would later realise this was a fierce platonic love – one borne of a friendship so strong that I couldn't reconcile it with the conventional parameters of friendship that I saw in films. But my desire was not for him. I liked him but I didn't want to be with him in that way. I just wanted to laugh with him and steal gin together.

Emily on the other hand was quite a different story.

I'd known her since we were twelve and sat together in the woodwind section of band where we both played saxophone. She'd left school but around seventeen came back and I felt myself, just like with Megan, emboldened by her. I stopped wearing the sports bra to flatten my chest and let the softness of my curves move freely under summer dresses.

At the first party of the summer I remember her speaking with my gin friend and there was a deep pit of anger in me. I raged until I realised it wasn't him I was jealous over. It was her. I wanted her. Emily and I drank vodka cranberries beside the fire and she dared me to kiss her. The hazy summer days turned into wild nights and we lay together in the night-dewed grass. At a party at her house we stole away together to a room full of dusty books and as we kissed her body tipped against the keys of an old out of tune piano and we laughed at its discordant symphony.

That summer in Blackwood would be the last time I would feel that kind of sweet joy and unrestrained excitement in my body for years.

Four years, now I come to think of it.

Glasgow

The welcome brochure had lied about Glasgow University. In the photographs the university swooned in a perpetual summer, the sky sharp blue with a single puffy cloud in the corner like one you'd draw in primary school except on one side it was tinged grey. Perhaps the cloud itself should have been an omen. Even in the most idealised, curated photograph they couldn't keep a speck of disharmony from appearing.

I thought that I might have a chance there. That I could cast the old version of myself off like a heavy coat in winter. That I could find some peace from the thoughts that plagued my days and haunted my nights.

I was wrong.

Glasgow University did not exist in a perpetual summer. Even now in August it was ringed in a strange orange hue, the black spires peaking into the matte sky. I walked through the entrance to find arcane cloisters like webbing from some ancient spider. And whatever it was that I sought – respite from the violent thoughts, a halfway normal life – it didn't exist here.

In the years following I would live in many parts of Scotland. Different cities and towns, out by the coast and in a tiny village in the shire, but as the old saying goes, 'Wherever you go, there you are.'

I couldn't escape myself.

But on that first day at Glasgow I still had a little hope. In the corridor of my dormitory I noticed a blonde girl trying to balance a box and suitcase at the same time. Her name was Imogen. When our eyes met I felt more calm than I had since leaving Blackwood. It was as if someone had turned off the radio static in my mind for a second. I was finally tuned to the right station. She smiled at me as if we were waving from two distant lighthouses to one another.

Oh look, I thought, it's my friend.

The summer air was pleasant on my skin as I walked with Imogen to the off-license (or 'liquor store' as one American in our dormitory had called it). With her by my side everything was brand new. The sun cast its last light across the city streets, transforming the banality of the scene – suits heading home from their city jobs, bohemian women riding bikes with baskets of fruit – into something beautiful. We found the off-licence. The shop had solid grates covering the alcohol so you had to point to the bottle you wanted to buy. The four walls were lined with dark green and purples bottles like an apothecary of old and I twitched in anticipation. Back at the dormitory Imogen taught me how to drink whiskey.

"Coleraine. It's from my hometown in Ireland," Imogen said pouring us glasses, her eyes lined with glitter shadow. "Don't worry I'll teach you how to drink it properly. First you have to sniff it, then take a sip – just a small sip – hold it in your mouth and *then* swallow."

The alcohol burned the soft pink of my mouth but when I swallowed it went down like sunshine. I thought I would always be able to rely on alcohol for some small respite from the obsessions, however brief that might be, but years down the line it would begin to fail me.

But at least for that night I had my whiskey and my friend and that was all I needed. As we got ready I stared at the same three outfits on the bed and wondered which Imogen might like best. I chose a green tea dress. One of the buttons at the chest was loose and I tried to thread it back on with the sewing kit from under the little sink in our room. I replaced the needles and recounted them, afraid that I might push them deep into the webbing of my toes. I took a razor over the bobbles of my tights and held back from pressing it deeper into my leg. I ran a wet comb through my hair to make it a little neater, careful to etch the part of my hair straight down the middle.

I'm pretending to be myself, I thought.

It had always been the same way. From a young age I had struggled with a restless self-consciousness. I was afraid to let people get too close in case somehow they could hear the violent thoughts that swarmed in my mind like agitated bees. It was as if I had a stain on me that others could see.

As a teenager I always felt dirty. The only time I didn't was that second after a bath or shower after I'd scrubbed my skin raw. One moment – then my feet would hit the bathmat and I'd be stained again.

That night as I dressed I felt a bit inferior in my cheap cloth coat like a shabby dormouse whose fur had rubbed till it was shiny and flat. I worried about summer's end for I knew as soon as it rained my shoes would let in water and my feet would never seem dry or warm again.

Imogen spotted a mark. A little smudged mascara. The cool of her hand cupped my chin and I was surprised by how gently she smoothed the make-up over my skin. She didn't use brushes but instead her fingers. I tried to hold fast and not flinch as I imagined her fingernails digging in.

Touch was a problem. The only kind I really tolerated well, sober, were hugs from my family but there was even a time limit for them, which if pushed past made me incredibly uncomfortable. It wasn't only myself I was afraid for. Sometimes with their limbs wrapped around me I could feel how easily I could snap them. Particularly with Lydia who was older than me but much smaller. In my mind I would hear the crunch of her tiny bird bones snapping and quickly withdraw from the hug. It became a lonely existence.

I yearned for touch and I found that alcohol went some way to stemming my discomfort. Times with Emily had always started with drinks. That night in Glasgow after a few I was able to link arms with Imogen and our dorm-mates as we walked up University Avenue to the Fresher party.

Behind the black gates callow undergraduates sat smoking on the stone wall bathed in the shifting neon lights. It seemed so strange to see the Victorian architecture lit up by the neon colours, the coarse carnival reds and purples making it seem more like a house of horrors than an antiquated place of learning. The gloaming upon us, Imogen and I and marched straight into the mouth of madness.

The first thing I noticed was the noise, although noise wouldn't have been the correct word for it. Onslaught, perhaps. The countryside slumber of my hometown had done little to prepare me for the vast swarm of people that buzzed in the club or the aching pound of music that reverberated in my skull.

Curiously though it didn't take long before my ears attuned to the cool ebb of the bass and the tension in my body left. Imogen winked at me and moved to fetch us drinks and I found myself cast into the middle of the crowd, and yet I wanted it. Part of me craved to be pulled apart atom by atom and to be lost in the dark crowd. Visions spun in my mind of an unknowable dark creature, what might seem to others a terrifying and huge black squid, pulsating and pulling me in with a lazy flick of its tentacles. I should be afraid, I thought. But the fear never came. Instead I clawed my way to the very centre of the crowd, looked the beast in the eye and let myself be subsumed by it.

We were one now.

The midnight hours came and went and left me drunk in their wake. A boy called Tommy who had long hair and a bright blue ring on his middle finger struck up a conversation with me at the bar. He reminded me of a pirate. The conversation blurred at the edges and I couldn't remember much of what I said or he said for that matter. I just remembered his eyes. The way they burned brightly as he looked at me. There was a thrill in the pit of my stomach at being seen. That night would be the last time I was free in this way. The last night before darkened bedrooms and rough and greedy hands.

Before they stole it from me.

Foxes

Autumn footed foxes crept around the city at night. I knew – I had seen them. Beautiful creatures with rakish grins and yellow eyes that peered back to me as if kin. These city foxes may have shared a genus with their country brothers but they were a different sort of creature. Even their physiology had adapted in their years of urban dwelling – their snouts longer for poking into rubbish bins and their fur shorter and coarser. Perhaps the most surprising change was in their personality. These foxes were bold. They lurked outside chip shops and clubs as if patrons themselves.

In Glasgow I was still a country fox. I had never gotten used to the city. In my first week during Freshers I had been fined by the police for drinking on the street. Naively, I hadn't known it was illegal. We drank in the street and the fields at home in Blackwood.

One night as I walked back to Kelvinhaugh dormitory after the club I noticed a city fox. Or rather he noticed me. He gambled behind, drafting me. Those large yellow eyes, reminiscent of some ancient earthly power, showed no fear. I tried to move closer but he cocked his head, raised one paw and then ran down the street.

The edges of my vision were soon obscured by a dark vignette. I'm still not sure why I hadn't gone back into the club. I had a habit of losing my friends. I wanted to become part of that anonymous shifting crowd where I didn't have to think anymore.

I tried to use my phone but I couldn't make sense of the screen or numbers. About two minutes away from my dorm I stumbled, trying to keep my limbs working properly. The edges grew darker.

I don't know where he came from.

"All alone, hen?"

I let out a nervous laugh. A man. A dark shape of a man, a much older man, drew into my vision. He pushed closer and I stepped away until I was backed against the wall. My whole body convulsed with fear, sheer adrenaline tearing through every fibrous nerve.

"Had a wee night out?"

His breath was sour. Greyscale tainted with beer and cigarettes.

"And you're all alone too?" His hands clutched my waist, pushing me into the wall. His eyes looked like two hollowed out sockets. A dead-eyed shark with rotting breath. I looked for someone who might help me but the street was empty.

"No, my boyfriend Richard is just up there getting cigarettes in the corner shop," I said.

His eyes shifted.

"Your boyfriend eh?"

"Yep. Just up there," I motioned, "I'd better go catch up with him before he worries."

"Richard?"

"Richard."

He shrugged.

"That's a shame hen, 'cos you're a pretty lass."

I giggled, desperate not to antagonise him.

He pulled back. As soon as he gave me an inch I ran across the road, not even bothering to check for incoming traffic, not caring if I got bludgeoned by a car. I ran to my dorm and collapsed on the floor of my dorm slick with sweat and nausea.

I tried my best to settle into life at Glasgow University but the truth was I never belonged there. The library was quiet and so I spent a lot of time there sitting between the shelves reading the titles. Words played like nursery rhymes in my brain and I used them to try to fill any space where obsessions might leak. Even while walking around campus I'd wear big headphones with blaring music to drown the thoughts out or I'd repeat, "Seven times seven is forty-nine," over and over. My favourite number of course.

But my concentration was failing. At the library the book I was reading didn't make sense. The letters squirmed like tiny bugs against the lemon chiffon pages and I rubbed my eyes only to find one of the squirming letters was a real bug.

I wandered home through the park in a nocturnal waltz, the thin limbs of the trees standing in a strict military parade, oblivious to my dance. When I reached Kelvinhaugh I got dressed for another party. Another night where I'd try to numb myself.

At the party I dragged a metal stool over to the kitchen and poured myself a quarter of the vodka bottle before anyone else noticed. A boy with a pinched face sat between two girls who tittered at every deeply unfunny thing he said. They must have been incredibly drunk. He caught me looking at him.

"So Jillian – I should call you Jilly – that's better. Little Jilly."

I focused on the centre of his brow so I didn't have to look him in the eye.

"I've been talking to the lads and we've a grand plan." His eyes darkened. "We thought how about Jamie here takes you in the back and sorts out that virginity for you?"

Everyone laughed. A pack of braying donkeys. But the boy with the pinched face didn't. He just watched me. My face flushed and I attempted to laugh but it came out as a snort which made his face twist in repellent glee. He enjoyed how uncomfortable I was. I noticed the girls beside him laughing and my heart sank. I wondered how it became them on one side of the room and me on the other.

I took another drink.

* * *

My best times were with Imogen. We danced together on nights out and she fed me sips of her drink like I was a little bird. I felt safe with her. Imogen and I created a space where we could be together. A boy called Harry transferred from the floor upstairs and I found another friend. He never judged me and had a dark sense of humour that kept me laughing into the night. He poured me shots of absinthe that tasted like peppermint and made my cheeks go numb.

Our nights together were my favourite.

The Gregory Building Statue, better known as The Stone Vagina, was an infamous sculpture many a drunken undergraduate had stood under. I was no different and took great delight in pretending to be birthed into the world.

"Having fun?" Imogen's eyes sparkled in a mischievous way.

"Endless. You should try it," I grinned.

"Oh I already have," Harry said laughing.

29

At that time in my life I just wanted to have fun with Imogen and Harry and live a normal life. My childhood or my dad weren't even in my thoughts. For all I'd been taught about seeing the patterns in life I couldn't divine the links from my past to my present. I thought the blame for any neurosis lay squarely on me. It was me who wasn't good enough.

Dirty, unclean.

Worthless.

And I knew it was just a matter of time before everyone found me out.

* * *

Though I loved Imogen and Harry, I still found myself drifting from them in the darkness of the clubs. One restless night out I found myself alone, again. Until I wasn't.

Gravity seemed to slow. I was at the very centre of the universe, the distant shapes around me like satellites, each spinning off. When I passed my fingers through the light it scattered so strangely. My body moved to the music; the notes bending past me.

He appeared beside me.

Tall with dark eyes. I could smell the leather of his jacket. I was so drunk the black filters crowded my vision. He crooked his head and smiled but there was no depth to his hollow eyes. He smoked a cigarette as we waited for a taxi. I held my shoes limply in one hand. The smoke billowed into the wine sky and he held me tightly at the waist.

In the taxi my head kept knocking against the window. My vision slowly tapered, the black blinds folding in. He steadied me and took me to my room. He pushed me onto the bed.

I didn't know how to tell him this had never happened before.

He was not kind to me.

He was frustrated that I was a virgin and got tired of waiting and so pushed himself in while I yelped and tried to get away.

He got what he wanted.

Afterwards I sat on the window ledge with my arms wrapped around my knees while he lay on the bed smoking. This wasn't how I thought it would go. My first time.

My head crashed against the window and this time I wished it would break my skull. In the morning I woke and distant images of the night returned. Bile rose in my throat. I turned and saw the grinning stranger in my bed, his mouth tainted from beer and cigarettes. My stomach twisted and I retched into the wastepaper basket. He shook his head in disgust and quickly made his exit.

I remember thinking, I'm left this way now. There was a before and now it can never be undone. I curled up in my bed but it didn't smell right anymore and so I stripped off the covers and threw them into the corner of the room. When it got dark I went to the bathroom and undressed. I held onto the sink and stared at my reflection. Mottled bruises covered my chest and thighs, cruel marks from tooth and hand. He kept hitting my face. He kept hitting my breasts. I never asked for any of it. The next day I covered the bruises under my eye and cheek with a thick layer of make-up. He had been rough with me and I was left torn inside. My hands shook as I put the stained tissues in the toilet where they bobbed like pink waterlilies. With disgust I turned away from the mirror and stepped into the shower, turning up the temperature to burn.

I wish this night had been my only experience like this.

Autumnal Burn

From the blackouts there are still some things that remain with me. Some memories I wish I could tear from my skin. In the dark of the club, blinded by alcohol, I couldn't see properly. I couldn't figure out how to open my eyes. There was someone beside me. They pulled me close to them on the dance floor. It was strange. There should have been music but I couldn't hear it. Instead there was a static roar, an absence of sound. I didn't recognise the man in front of me but he pulled me closer. Reality fragmented and memories reduced to stills in my mind. A frame of the stairs, the taxi, an unknown bed and an unknown body.

I don't want this.

Please.

But I couldn't keep my eyes open and my words slurred backwards.

Just let me sleep.

Please.

I'm so tired.

But he didn't want that. He wanted more and I couldn't form the sound to make him stop. He pushed me onto my front.

He pulled my tights and underwear down and my legs apart. He unfastened his belt and forced himself into me anally. I stayed limp like a rag doll.

The frame ended.

The next day I bled again.

Tiny fissures.

I couldn't sit down without becoming slick with sweat.

* * *

The death of summer was abrupt.

Autumn turned the trees in the park almond and amber and I would sit in the painted hall in the university and think how lovely it was. The spires stretched on to the very heavens themselves, the ribbed vaults were reminiscent of a chapel, imbuing the air with a certain holiness. I could look upon those structures for hours and still never fully discover their secrets.

I had enough secrets of my own locked away.

Glasgow was one of the best universities in the country and yet I was miserable there. Somehow the stone was too heavy and I couldn't seem to breathe without dust catching in my lungs. It was as if I were one of the statues, my skin growing paler until cracks began to line it like fine porcelain, my eyes closed as if half caught in a dream.

The university was so entirely disconnected from the real world that most of the time I felt like goldfish bumping my head against the glass of the bowl. I never thought I'd be so sheltered from certain social realities, so far removed from any real meaning or connection. I felt like screaming, *What is the point?*

In dusty lecture theatres I tried to stay present but Professor Robertson's words became muffled. He was an older man with curly hair that greyed at the temples and a cardigan just worn enough to look vintage without him seeming untidy. He paused after sentences just a little too long as if he were hoping for it to bring more potency to his words, but it just made me feel uneasy.

"There will never be another time like this in your whole life," Professor Robertson said standing with a practised nonchalance and one hand in his pocket. "You can't imagine how lucky you are. To be at this school and spend your days where so many have come before you."

I was wary of people who decided which would be my best days. The same line had been parroted by my high school teachers and I had thought then, *If these are truly the best days of my life then I might as well end it now.*

Robertson gave me an A on an assignment – an oral presentation on a book I had obviously never read. I would see him outside his office talking with female undergraduates, always standing just a little too close. In seminars I felt an untethered rage rise up trapped in that small room with him and would have to sit on my hands as thoughts of tearing my nails down his face flooded my mind. I could almost feel the way his flesh would gather under my nails.

I had the privilege of attending university and all I thought was, *I'm taking someone else's place.* It shamed me to feel so little, to be reduced to a statistic and placed in a frame that focused on grades at the expense of any deeper learning. It strangled all passion and my once steadfast love for literature withered. There was a new leaden tiredness from constantly being in the company of other people. With my defences breached it became difficult to stave off the obsessions and so I sought distraction of any kind.

Alcohol is quite the distraction.

In the Tarot there is a minor arcana card known as the Nine of Cups. Its artwork changes depending on the deck but it nearly always has golden cups and a swirling background of colour symbolising a great swell of decadence. This is the image that swims in my mind as I remember those first few months at Glasgow.

We were first years and so we drank; it was the natural thing to do. How many others were using alcohol in the same way as I was – to blunt some psychological trauma? I didn't know. I was only concerned about myself and where my next drink was coming from.

My own routine soon formed. Two bottles of white wine before the club. Every place was different and exactly the same. Some were darker and cramped and some were under railway stations and housed art during the day. It didn't really matter. Once I arrived I would head straight to the bar and order two drinks to keep from sobering up.

The dulling effect of the loud music and alcohol on the obsessions was perfect. The violent images lost their potency and I often blacked out and wasn't in my head at all. This kind of oblivion was everything I sought. Strangely, I never bothered with drugs of any other kind. I didn't see the point when I had alcohol. Perhaps this was for the best – knowing where alcohol alone would lead me.

At the club I'd have maybe fifteen or more drinks of vodka and whichever mixer was cheapest. The cranberry juice didn't taste as sweet as last summer. Before long I ditched mixers and drank my vodka straight. Club vodka tastes like battery acid.

My friends and I went out four nights a week. Saturdays were the worst in town so we skipped them to stay in and play our own games. Nights in meant dark rum. If I was low on money, which was usually the case, I got the cheapest white label vodka the supermarket offered. I'd get through a third of vodka when writing an essay or a bottle or two of red wine which invariably gave me vampire mouth. Rarely I bought a pack of beer. The volume of alcohol required to feel even a slight buzz annoyed me. But if there was nothing else available I enjoyed sitting at my desk and tipping the beer bottle and watching the foam creep up the side. I longed for a moment of amnesia, to pour bleach on my brain, and the solvency of alcohol suited that purpose remarkably well. The recommended weekly alcohol consumption is fourteen units.

I was getting through over one hundred and fourteen.

There was also a compulsive element when I touched myself. Before there had been a dark excitement in the pit of my stomach as I explored my body and remembered scenes from static television screens late at night. That was gone now and replaced by a restlessness. A gnawing hunger that could never be satiated no matter how hard I tried. My first experiences of sex were abusive and so I tried to mimic it by hitting myself in the face and scratching my legs. This wasn't me playing with boundaries and taboos in a healthy way – I was trying to hurt myself. Years later I would understand that control and relinquishing it could play a beautiful part in the bedroom between two people. But for now I was left wanting with white light flashing before my eyes as I hit myself over and over again. I was trying to snatch some dopamine, some feel good neurochemical that would give me respite from the violence for a time.

But it never came.

* * *

I kept the truth of what was happening at Glasgow to myself. I never told anyone. I created a lovely illusion for everyone. It was like finding a rare print of art in a charity shop and flipping it over to find flecks of mould that marred the back. On closer inspection you could see the frame had been warped by the same damp. The same rot was within me. The print of a young woman

36

thriving in her first year of university, settled into her new accommodation, with good marks and friends and a family she returned home to every Sunday for lunch. This was the lie.

On the underside lay the rot.

My drinking had spiralled out of control and I wasn't sleeping. Robertson's morning seminars were traded in favour of dark dancehalls the night before. Nightmares soon became night terrors and my body untethered itself as I sleepwalked and woke screaming. At 3am I would run to the bathroom and pull down the waterline of my eye to check it was not puckered with holes where insects might burrow.

The thoughts were getting worse.

One day while in the shower I put some hair removal cream on my vulva and then before I could think I had pushed some of the cream inside my vagina.

Dirty.

I quickly washed the chemicals away but for the next few days my vagina burned. Yet some part of me took a perverse satisfaction in the pain. The chemical burns meant I might finally be clean.

At Kelvinhaugh in the kitchen there was a small set of knives from IKEA with each of the handles painted the colours of the rainbow. The red one was the sharpest. I stole it from the set and made sure the door was locked. I rolled down my tights and pressed the blade across the pale flesh of my leg. I was only skimming at first until I realised nothing was happening apart from a few white marks. So I pierced deeper. The pink swelled into a red blossom. I stared at the drops of blood. The dark static flooded my brain, incomprehensible, but it was as if the sharp pain blocked out any thoughts. I had just found another coping mechanism.

Blood was the solution.

Winter Sowing

A new obsession took hold.

Red.

Every morning I would wake with a start and desperately run my hands over my underwear – my mind wracked with images of ripping and tearing. I pressed my legs together so tightly they left red marks. Compulsions are as insidious as obsessions. Though I would tell myself not to, I couldn't stop myself from waking every morning and performing my checks. It's as if my hands were possessed. If I tried not to check I would feel a screaming pressure in my skull. After all, in the moment of waking my mind truly believed that I would find my vagina torn and blood in my underwear – how could you not check?

This is perhaps one of the sickest jokes of OCD. I could see how irrational I was being and yet in the moment the fear was so real to me. It warped my reality. However, compulsions did not give me lasting resolution. Each time they became less and less effective and so I performed them more like a drug addict needing more of a substance to chase that first high.

Or an alcoholic.

The ill effects of alcohol were skewing my internal chemistry. It fuelled my paranoia. It deepened the depressive wave I found myself caught in. So many of my friends spoke of 'the fear' after drinking and I wondered how we all normalised the crushing anxiety that we woke with in the morning after a night out.

The obsessions held me hostage and I stopped going to class. I'd hold my hand over my underwear and shake my head to try and erase the images like an etch-a-sketch.

My bedroom was freezing. The winter sun was rimmed by a sharp glass film, the heat refracting through clear and cold. Winter was crystalline in its beauty. It had always been my favourite season. But this year was different. There were no stars to be found in the city sky – in their place only lightless tracts. They had forgotten me. The dark hours passed and I stared at the ceiling entombed in my own mind.

The red topped knife I had stolen was my only companion. A blossom of blood stained through my shirt and my arms and knees were littered with fresh wounds that didn't seem to heal.

I was frightened to go outside of my room. My friends would leave sweets and cans of juice outside my door as if offerings to an otherworldly spirit who survived on sugar and caffeine. My world had shrunk. I would stay under my covers with my laptop and watch documentaries to have some dialogue that wasn't my own thoughts.

There was one documentary on life inside a mental hospital. Like a nervous bird I eyed the screen sideways. The story followed different patients in their day to day lives. One man called John had schizophrenia and depression. With a glowing pride he showed the filmmakers his room and adjusted his glasses and said, "So that's me. I keep myself square. I used to get such bad thoughts. Things got really bad. But we all go through hard times and if there's something I know it's that people can get through a fair lot. There's always something to keep going for." He nodded towards a nurse who beamed back at him with such affection.

A seed became rooted in my mind.

I acted quickly. Online I searched for available courses and picked the one furthest away. In forty minutes I had written my personal statement and arranged a meeting with my course advisor for the next day.

"So Mental Health Nursing?" she said.

"Yes. It probably seems a bit out of nowhere but –"

She waved her hands. "You don't need to explain to me. I went from Engineering to English. People try lots of different things before they find the one that fits."

My advisor was kind and I left her office with a recommendation despite being strangers. I followed the path through Kelvingrove Park and sat on a frosted bench. At dusk a friend joined me. I couldn't be sure it was the fox from before but it didn't matter. I locked eyes with the creature. Those large yellow eyes peered back at me. I felt a kinship with the fox. We shared something. A rootlessness. A dislocation that had been with me as far back as I could remember.

That weekend I visited Mama, Lydia and Jim. The cherry tree in our front garden had lost all its leaves.

"Don't worry darling. It's just in dormancy. We all need a little rest from winter," Mama said while pulling me into a hug.

"All its blossom has gone," I said.

"Yes, but cherry trees are adapted to colder climates – this is all part of its natural cycle. This part is just as important."

I hid my depression from my family. I was careful to wear thick tights and long-sleeved tops to mask the cuts on my arms and knees. Winter made this easier. If my family suspected anything I didn't know. I pretended everything was fine. We curled up on the couch together and watched television and I'd have to stop myself twitching from obsessions. I had bad headaches.

Mama kissed me goodnight and though I was eighteen she tucked me into my old bed with its mismatched covers and kissed my forehead. I felt swaddled like a baby. Safe. That night I had some respite from the nightmares and instead dreamed of a labyrinth of tunnels below Glasgow, underground dens where city foxes slept. On Sunday morning Mama cooked breakfast and made sure I ate some fresh fruit.

I wanted to stay.

There are marks in time like grooves on a vinyl record that I wish I could push the needle into. The what ifs. What if instead of faking a smile at the station I had told Mama what was going on in? What if we'd driven to the hospital and asked to see a psychiatrist? What if I had come home and stayed with Mama, Jim and Lydia in Blackwood and gotten better? What if I had never left?

But the record never plays a different song.

I didn't tell her. I kissed Mama's soft cheek goodbye and left part of myself behind in the car with her. I got on the train. In the carriage I cried as the beeping noise of the doors signalled them closing. I felt hope leave me. But perhaps the needle was in the right place after all and the path it followed was one that was inevitable, fated, because if I hadn't gone to the sea, if I hadn't gone to Dundee – I would never have had the chance to die.

Last Summer

The indolence of summer passed me by. Instead of stepping in time with its slow, heady days I became frenetic like an agitated insect, unable to rest in one place for too long. Drinking more. Spending more money on alcohol and pretty dresses. The payments to cover living expenses stopped during the summer so I got a job at a call centre. I wasn't very helpful on the phone and constantly put people on hold to look up information on the database. But there was a small bit of beauty in that summer job – I made friends. Ross from Castlemilk who had a sardonic grin permanently etched across his face and Leo a poet with long hair who did open mic nights at the weekend. After another terrible call they would give me little thumbs up of encouragement. They took care of me. They made me laugh. They made the days bearable.

One weekend I woke to the summer heat and grabbed my phone to see if I had any new messages.

I had a new addiction.

His name was Eli.

The first time I met him was in a club. Under the green neon lights he looked like a hungry ghost with shadows under his eyes. The next time we met I couldn't catch my breath as I walked through the balmy city. I was excited, terrified. Strangely at ease with my unease. The heat pressed close. There were no wildflowers in the city. In their place were neatly curated gardens with summer drenched flowers weeks past their fresh bloom.

In the tangerine dusk he took my hand. We spent the night in his favourite bar drinking sweet rum and ginger and told each other our stories. We kissed in the summer rain while everyone around us ducked into bars for shelter. I had never felt so high. I walked home and the lights of the clubs reflected in the inky waters of the streets. Swirls of jet and neon shone in my eyes. One word consumed every electrified fibre of my being.

Eli.

On waking from a sweet rum hangover the following day, I found an acceptance letter from Dundee University to study Mental Health Nursing. It surprised me because I didn't think my interview had gone so well – I had gotten two of the faces mixed up in the emotional recognition test.

I celebrated with my friends and white wine. The July heat made the street buzz with frenetic energy. Little pockets of people with golden pints of beer milling outside the pub. I thought of messaging Eli but since I was leaving, what was the point? I couldn't have him so the summer night and some wine would have to do.

But there might as well have been a cardboard cut-out version of myself parading around the party. Hollow sentiments slipped from my mouth with each sip of drink. I don't know who I was pretending to be. To gasps of horror, I stumbled across the room and crashed face first into the radiator. Harry picked me up and asked if I was okay. Cartoon birds buzzed around my head and I burst out laughing. I was too numb and too stupid from the alcohol to realise I had been mere inches away from fracturing my cheekbone.

Though I was leaving and our relationship was finite I knew I had to see Eli again. The next time I met him the make-up I'd applied didn't quite cover the darkening bruise from the radiator. I tried to make a joke of it but he didn't seem to find it all that funny.

That last summer before Dundee was only Eli. The city blurred as the taxi sped through streets dappled in pale neon. My chest ached when I climbed out and saw him and his dark eyes lined with shadows. He would pull me close and for a moment I felt whole. Let time fracture and this be it, I thought. We walked through the city together. We kissed on the cobbled steps and talked until the dawn spilled the city blue. The city was two dimensional and we were the only real, solid things.

But I couldn't give him anything.

Every part of me was locked away and I couldn't let anyone in. Not even him. When his fingers traced the patterns on my tights I would push him away.

"Hey don't worry, there's no rush okay?" Eli said.

When we kissed he held my face as if I was as fragile as gossamer. He was kind but when he left in the morning I was left hating myself for the things I couldn't do and the things I couldn't feel anymore.

Red.

Flashes of other nights. Of other bodies.

I yearned to cast off my body and step into another, one without memory.

The last time I saw Eli we sat at the bar and he simply held my hand as I rested my head on his shoulder. When it came down to it there wasn't much that needed to be said. I had nothing to give him save for a few fragments of myself. No

44

grand ending – just two souls that rested in each other's company for a while.

We headed back to my room and he pulled me into bed and I tried to let what I felt for him take hold but when his hands moved further down I froze.

Red.

Memories of shadowy rooms. My body remembered the sharp splintering and severance of myself. It didn't matter how I felt about Eli or how much I wanted him – I couldn't. In bed he held me and I stared at the ceiling. His face was half cut in shadow but I could still make out his eyes. In the morning he left.

All that's left of him now are a few songs in an old playlist.

With Eli gone and my few boxes packed I took my final exams at Glasgow University. It was pointless to even go but I scribbled nonsense in my book until the clock chimed and I could leave with the first wave of students. In the cloisters I thought of sitting on the bench for a while, to take it in one last time, but I had nothing left in my heart for that place. For all its beauty it didn't make sense. I walked past the black gates and felt the swell of a strange tide ahead of me.

The sea called me.

St Michaels

I had never lived beside the sea before. Lydia drove me from one city to another and I believed I would get better there. A dormitory called Seabraes was my new home; it was a block of student flats not far from campus and situated a small and happy distance from the water. I was roughly two hours away from the part of the country I had lived my whole life. There was a blanket horizon of possibility waiting and I was desperate to take it all in – or be taken in.

There was a manic edge to my move. I thought that I could lose myself in a new place with new people. I bought the strongest peroxide I could find and dyed my hair in the tiny bathroom while inhaling the noxious fumes. With the last copper tones rinsed out I found the bleach had left my hair a white blonde colour. My skin was too pale against the white hair. It was as if the portrait of the girl had been soaked in turpentine and bleached of all identifying characteristics. This suited me. I wanted to be rid of the stain on me. A ghost with blank eyes stared through the mirror and I thought, fine, let it kill who I was before.

After a second Freshers fraught with excess and a sense of futile repetition I began my Mental Health Nursing degree at Dundee University.

The hospital loomed in front of me on my first day on placement. Grand and terrifying. Earlier that morning I had pulled on my light blue scrubs and scrubbed my face until it was fresh and pink. From the city I took the train across the water to Fife and when it careened over the bridge I was sure it would break and that my fellow sleepy passengers and I were about to plunge to our doom.

The hospital was called St Michaels. My mentor had tired eyes and led me through the motions with a dull affect. We stepped through a large arched corridor into a room with cracked leather armchairs all facing a television. A garishly bright morning show played and patients stared without really watching. The burgundy carpet was stained and frayed and had little rugs tossed over the worst parts.

My mentor introduced me to the patients. One girl called Elsie who had bent metal frame glasses and a purple fleece smiled at me from her seat and I beamed back. The residents looked tired. In the nurses station equally weary women sat in mottled chairs.

Except they wore uniforms.

* * *

"I'll kill you! You fucking whore!" Margaret screamed as her arm struck out at me.

After the first time I caught a blow to the side of my head I had quickly learned to duck Margaret's punches. I casually dodged her arm and continued feeding her though I knew she didn't like the congealing grey gloop they called porridge very much. Or me, for that matter.

I had been at St Michaels a month.

The hospital itself was set up in old Victorian houses that had been divided into different wards and was surrounded by little square gardens with oddly stiff ornaments. In Blackwood people had statues of goblins and wizards in their gardens which from the corner of your eye seemed to spring in and out of their cast stone form on a whim.

But not at St Michaels.

I could never get over the strange silent grounds and stone houses where patients milled about and muttered bleakly to themselves. I spent most of my time with Greta. She was elderly and confined to her bed and had no hair except for a tuft at the side of her head like a small puff of white smoke. Her breathing was laboured and dragged. At busy mealtimes I escaped the noise of the cafeteria and hung out with Greta – feeding her mashed potato with a blue plastic spoon.

During the day when she was awake I'd bring her lemonade in a sippy cup or sit beside her and look out at the salted grey sky that joined with the grey buildings to form an impenetrable wall. I fixed the flickering signal on her television and we watched shows together. Greta probably knew I wasn't great at being a nurse but she was always kind to me. When she could focus she looked at me with a keen familiarity as if I were someone she knew.

In the mornings the patients lined up for their medication and I lined up beside them. They told me about their plans for the day and who was going to the shop for a roll and crisps and who was going to take a bath. Sometimes the line was a lot shorter and missing patients who hadn't managed to make it out of bed usually appeared later at dinner, slumping at the table, their eyes dark and heavy. I'd gently ask them how they were doing and they'd try to focus on me and then shake their heads.

At St Michaels another piece of me splintered off.

For the most part the patients seemed to like me. They smiled and waved at me in the corridors and I was often the one they'd ask for their cigarettes knowing I'd give them out early. I'd sit with them while they bathed and chattered happily and then I'd make sure they were properly dry and rubbed moisturiser over their sore bits. In the afternoons I would dry and straighten patients' hair in the corridor. One day while smoothing one lady's flyaways she cupped my face in her wrinkled hands and said, "Angel. You've come back."

I felt more at home with the patients than I did with the nurses. Eventually I got a tour of everyone's room. Elsie introduced me to her stuffed animal collection and Jenny showed me the chocolates she kept for the nurses.

Of course there was the occasional incident. One time a patient hissed that she was going to murder me but I just nodded and slunk out of the room with my hand on my alarm. It was clear she wasn't having a very good day and the sight of my face wasn't helping that. Another night I was out with two senior nurses doing a sweep of the hospital. We were looking for an escaped patient from a neighbouring ward. As I walked around the haunted grounds with my flashlight barely making a dent in the darkness I tried to stifle a laugh at how bizarre it all felt.

One day Elsie asked if I'd like to go with her to the cafe and we bought packets of salt and vinegar crisps and Irn-Bru and ate them on the bench. Elsie was having a day where her thoughts and speech were muddled and I knew she just needed some companionship.

The next day I was walking along the corridor when I saw Elsie facing the wall, her fingers tracing the pattern of the faded wallpaper.

"Elsie?"

She didn't respond. I touched her gently on the shoulder and she looked at me with unfocused eyes, drooling. Her speech was broken and I could only catch a word here and there. As she turned I realised she was wet.

"Elsie we need to change you, darling. You've had a wee accident but it's okay. Everything is okay."

Her face crumpled and she wailed and started clawing at her wet trousers. In the nearest bathroom I ran a bath. Elsie was crying and shaking. The howls that were coming from her were unbearable. She yelped like an animal in pain.

Red.

I shook my head to try and stop the thoughts.

"We're going to get you all better Elsie, okay? We'll get you dry and warm. You're safe I promise."

She howled. I helped her out of her sodding wet clothes and into the tub, the water splashing over the sides. Once she was in the water her cries stopped. She was completely still, her wide eyes looking in wonder at the bubbles floating above her.

"You are okay, Elsie. You are safe."

She turned her wide eyes to me and pointed to my scrubs.

"Ummm... bubbles."

I looked down and saw the bubbles on my scrubs and smiled.

"You're right Elsie, lovely bubbles!"

She opened her mouth in a wide grin and then her whole expression softened and she leaned back in the tub. We spent the afternoon like that. When required I added more hot water to the bath but mostly I just listened as she babbled away in half formed sentences and giggled, her hands splashing gently in the water.

I began to lose all sense of time and it was Phillip Schofield's fault. I came to loathe his face. He was a British presenter who not only had a morning show, but an afternoon show and some quiz programme at night. No matter the time of day there he'd be – his face laced with a tight grin and the studio lights reflecting off his silver cap of hair.

St Michaels was full of televisions. There wasn't enough money for resources to help the patients and so they were fobbed off with screens. The few occupational therapist visits we had I got to see the ladies shine. We did art therapy together and they told me about their lives. I ended up with an arm full of plastic beaded friendship bracelets. We did physical therapy with resistance bands although it proved quite the task to stop the ladies from pinging the bands at each other. In the end no one really followed the routine but we bopped along quite happily to the music for a bit.

I swayed with them and tried to distract myself from the truth.

The thoughts were only getting worse.

Life inside and outside of the hospital was becoming unbearable. St. Michaels was not separate from the living world but a concentrated, amplified version of it. I cared for the ladies and yet it was never enough because I couldn't reconcile the fact that I got to leave at the end of the day and they were left locked up behind me.

I grew weary of the smell of carbolic soap and sadness that filled the ward. Of the musty clothes and slack jaws of the ladies when they were given too much medication. I brushed Greta's tuft of hair and wondered how I would feel if this was the end of my life. She had been known to try to choke herself on her fruit pastilles and so I had to carefully watch her swallow each one.

Red.

At St Michaels we put up the Christmas decorations. The tree slumped to one side like a crooked old man but it brought a little cheer to the usually drab television room. The patients helped hang up dusty baubles and chirped about Christmas

51

lunch. We toasted each other with orange juice in little paper cups and I affected an expression I hoped was more grin than grimace as I tried to hold my juice down. My drinking was getting worse. I was blacking out half the week. In the middle of the night I rushed to the bathroom and spat up acid. It came in pulsing streams, burning my throat and making my eyes water.

Every morning I woke up wishing I hadn't. I would lie in bed staring despondently at the ceiling and then pace up and down the corridors at St Michaels desperate for my mind to stop plaguing me.

Red.

The sound of metal scraped through the hollows of my mind and I would see Lydia's mangled body after a car accident.

I made sure to include in every text message after:

"Please drive safe."

Red.

Mama's cracked skull and lifeless eyes.

I became obsessed with telling her how to step in and out of the shower a certain way so she didn't slip and get hurt.

The thoughts were relentless.

I saw my family burned. I saw their skin peeled back from their faces. Their howls of pain rang in my ears. Waves of nausea passed through me and though I tried to stay present and enjoy the Christmas cheer with the sweet patients at St Michaels the fluorescent lights were too yellow, too hot.

When my shift ended I could still smell the hospital.

Dundee

Daylight radiated into the room. My hands passed over my cotton underwear as the world slowly shifted into focus. I had no idea where I was. A bed. Someone beside me. The unfamiliar became strangely familiar. I pulled myself up and tried to stop my hands from shaking. My mouth tasted like tar. I quietly collected my clothes spread around the room and closed the door behind me.

The sea air knocked my head as I walked along the pavement still drunk from the night before. People passed by. Odd shapes with inexplicable expressions. I wondered if I could touch them. If they were real. I chased after a seagull who looked deeply unimpressed.

At Seabraes I turned on music and stripped off my clothes. I sat down in the shower with my eyes closed letting the waves of searing hot water numb me. My fingers traced bruises on my breasts, my thighs, my arms. I thought if I turned up the water hot enough that it might flay the first layer of my skin off.

Every night was meant to be the last but somehow I kept waking up.

At the seafront I watched boats cast off and shrink like opal gems into the horizon. I wondered where they might end up. Dundee was meant to be where I started again, where I got better, but I only grew more unstable. My obsessions burned in the raw daylight and bled into my dreams. I found myself caught in a hopeless cycle of anxiety and depression. I would work during the week at St Michaels and then on the weekends I'd drink.

Then there were the unfamiliar beds with strangers.

When I was drunk I had no sense of danger. In clubs I'd meet people and go home with them. I'd sit on dilapidated couches with people around me doing drugs. One time I talked all night to a poor guy because he had been jumped and punched in the head and his friends didn't want him falling asleep if he had a concussion. During sex I'd push people away if they tried to go down on me. I was terrified of their mouths being that close. I became convinced they would sink their teeth into my vagina. Rip and tear the soft flesh. In dark bedrooms I was nothing more than a hollow void to be filled. I wouldn't be able to leave until I "did that again," with an arm like a vice around me. Even if I were able to get out, I had no idea where I was. So I stayed.

I had one friend called Jack who was also a student nurse. Jack was six foot four and what some might call a typical 'lad' but that was just a veneer. Underneath the bravado he was kind. Sometimes I saw him with his guy friends adopting the same sexist and misogynist jokes and I thought, I can see right through you. He was playing a part, trying to affect the same mannerisms and style as the group because like all of us he just wanted to be accepted. Looking back we gravitated towards one another because of a shared kind of brain chemistry. And of course a shared addiction. We were complicit in each other's drinking.

My paranoia grew like a festering wound. Everything took on a nightmarish quality. Distorted faces crushed in beside me at the traffic light crossing. It was as if they were wearing hideous masks. The red noise in my mind and the colours of the traffic lights blurred together until I found myself in the middle of the road with the screech of a car ringing in my ears and the driver shaking his head at me.

The salted wind tore at my face as I wandered into the night, drunk again. Looking again. I was desperate to find some experience – something real. But it never came.

At the seafront I sat on a bench and tried to focus on a family in knitted jumpers that looked straight out of an M&S advert. Their kids were playing by the dolphin bollards. They were chasing each other, weaving in and out of the marine creatures, giggling.

But not even this innocuous moment was safe.

The jagged edge of violent thoughts bled in and I was shown the children with their faces gouged.

I quickly left the bench.

The following Friday I decided it was time to go.

After my afternoon lecture there was a student in front of me who kept shouting over the crowd to his friend. I wanted to grab his head and smash it repeatedly into the desk. My fingers gripped the desk. Tiny little staves drove their way into my fingertips. I rested my head in my hands and tried to block out as much of the noise as I could. Jack's concerned face blurred into vision and he asked if I was okay. I told him I was just tired and was going to go home that weekend. He nodded before asking again if I was okay.

I promised him I was.

On my way back from the university I stopped at the off-license and bought wine and vodka. I drifted back to Seabraes and locked my door. I stayed there all weekend drinking and eyeing the paracetamol I had collected but I didn't take them. Instead I drank the vodka and wine and lay down on the thin carpet of my dorm room. The tides of my mind were black.

The dark was pierced by a frantic call from Jack.

"Please come upstairs. Please."

I unfolded my limbs of stone and went upstairs and he answered the door before I could even knock. His eyes were filled with tears. I didn't understand what was happening. Jack said he wanted to check on me so he messaged home and when Mama said I wasn't there, everyone had gotten really worried.

My stomach lurched and I could taste metal. I felt sickened that I had upset my family and Jack like that. Mama phoned but years later I can't remember what we said to each other. How did I explain? Was I honest with her?

I don't know.

Jack promised everything would be okay. He had spoken to the university and started looking for flats for us for second year. He said he'd take care of me. That he'd do anything. I just had to stay and he'd make it okay.

I didn't deserve a friend like him.

The university lecturer for my course visited me at St Michaels. She asked how I was doing and studied my face. I told her I was doing great. She said she had no doubt and that she'd heard great things about me from the nurses. But, she hesitated, they weren't daft, they knew most people get into this line of work because they know mental illness in some kind of way.

I was blank. I truly didn't understand what she was trying to say.

After my lecturer left I reported to the nurses station where my mentor and I had the same chat. She said I was good with the patients and had all the qualities of a great nurse, but then she sighed and said something that would always stay with me:

"But we have to take care of ourselves before we can take care of anyone else."

She took my hand and told me it was vital that I get the help I need right now.

I stared at the carpet. I couldn't meet her eyes.

My shift ended and back at Seabraes I curled into a small ball in the middle of the floor.

The next morning at the station my card was declined and I knew it was over.

I didn't go back to St Michaels.

I called in sick and cobbled enough change together to buy wine using the self-service machine. The rest of the week I tried to scrape enough money together for alcohol. It was a good day when I found some silver coins. They eventually ran out too. I stole food from the communal kitchen in my dormitory and ignored their messages. One night, drunk, I opened the window in the kitchen and it came out of its hinges and nearly broke my foot. I just left it like that. My roommates were furious but I didn't care. St Michaels phoned and I ignored their calls. The university phoned and I ignored their calls. I passed the hours in my room with the curtains drawn and became very still when anyone knocked on my door and prayed for them to go away. Waking from night terrors, my eyes mistook the lights for hundreds of tiny spiders parachuting down from their webs. When I tried to catch them in my hands they disappeared.

My mind was trying to kill me.

Hungry ghosts lurked around the city of Dundee. Their eyes orange and their cloaks a shroud. I was between worlds and I couldn't get back to the light. The ghosts were hidden in plain sight, standing in the fountain, their eyes cool on me. They welcomed me. And part of me wanted to join them. Part of me wanted to die.

I wanted to die because I didn't understand this place anymore.

The world was too violent and sad and I couldn't live with the fear. At night I couldn't stop thinking. It was as if my mind was engraving every atrocity in the world on the plates of my skull. If there was any beauty left in the world I couldn't see it and I certainly couldn't feel it.

I wanted to go to sleep.

For a very long time.

At the train station I stood close to the edge. In my mind I always jumped.

When I was younger in Blackwood and struggling with the obsessions there was still hope. I used to feel myself stretch beyond this body and its blood. I was sure there was something more.

That was gone now.

In my bed at Seabraes I tried to sleep but when I closed my eyes the thoughts pierced through. In my mind I saw a baby cooing with its tiny hands kept safe in its soft sleep-suit.

I smiled.

Perhaps tonight was different. A little respite.

But it was never different.

It always turned.

Red.

The baby lay decapitated. The torn flesh of its neck wept blood. Greasy white spinal fluid like a caterpillar trail. A dark hollow.

I shook my head but the baby didn't go away. I opened my eyes but it didn't go away. I thought of blades and pills and a thousand other ways to silence my mind for the final time. I couldn't live like this anymore. I needed to get out but in my irrational panic I thought that Mama might not understand.

Being a failure in her eyes terrified me. Especially after already having dropped out once.

Of course if I had been honest with Mama and Lydia and told them what was happening maybe things would have turned out differently. They would have taken care of me. They might not have understood in the beginning, and they might have been a little afraid, but we could have made it work.

Maybe.

Maybe then I wouldn't have ended up contacting the one person I definitely shouldn't have.

My dad.

Hamilton

"We're the same – you and I."

That's what my dad always said.

At Seabraes I logged onto Facebook and sent him a message telling him I was desperate and needed a place to stay. Three dots in the chat bubbled and then: "I'll sort out the room. Does your mum know?"

She didn't.

When I told Lydia and her, they were angry but only because they were confused. My behaviour seemed erratic. They knew I was anxious and often depressed but they had no idea how far it had gone. And they certainly had no idea about my obsessions. They thought I should stay on in Dundee and come back in three years once I'd finished my degree.

I'd be dead in three years.

They just wanted what was best for me. Most of all they wanted me to be happy. When they asked me questions I would sit in silence unable to find the words to describe what was happening my mind. How would they have reacted if I'd been flatly honest? *"Mama, Lydia – I'm going mad."* The thing is, I'll never know.

Jack dropped me off at Dad's flat in Hamilton. He had tried to convince me to stay but it was too late. Dad cleared a room and left me a little camp bed to sleep in. The floorboards sagged in places and the gaps between were like rotten teeth. Old nails stuck up from some of the floorboards but I soon created a safe path where I dodged splinters and resisted the urge to push my feet down on the rusty nails.

That first night tucked up in the camp bed I let myself cry. The next day Dad made me go into town to get food and cleaning supplies. I tried to explain how tired and anxious I was but he didn't listen. He pushed me on the bus instead and in the shop I followed him mutely like I was six years old again.

I had no money. I had no job. I was entirely dependent on him for everything and that made me nervous. I signed on for Jobseeker's Allowance and waited in a room with little plastic seats until a thin woman waved me over, the gold bracelets on her wrists clinking against one another in a little jingle. Everything in the room was grey. Grey box furniture. Grey filing cabinets. Grey walls. She seemed too bright for such a room.

"No need to look so worried, pet," she said and gave me an encouraging smile.

Each week I kept to my appointments at the Jobcentre and showed them my booklet with positions I'd applied for. I hadn't heard back from anyone. No phone calls or emails. Humiliation burned my insides but I wasn't surprised. I was a two-time university drop-out with no skills or experience and a brain full of worms.

There didn't seem to be a way out.

The edges between night and day became so blurred I could hardly tell the difference. I performed my checking

61

compulsions after waking in the fetid room, terrorised in the night by a man who sliced through my ankle bone with a hacksaw and hammered nails into my face.

Every night I died and every morning I was resurrected and made to live through the same waking nightmare. In the mirror I'd constantly check there were no holes in the waterline of my eyes from bugs burrowing in. I kept a baseball bat near the door so I could cave in the head of anyone who tried to hurt me. In the little camp bed, I'd lie on my side with my hands on my chest trying to stop it from cleaving open. There wasn't a hob or oven so my diet consisted of ready meals and sandwiches. I moved an old television into the room. A distant hum to keep me company.

Dad worked during the day at the hospital and watched television while napping on the couch at night. He didn't want to be around me. One rare night he said we could watch a television show together but he stumbled into the flat six hours later smelling like the pub and asked if we could do it some other time. We never did. Before I could get out of the room he said, "Come give your old dad a hug."

Dad only gave hugs when he was drunk. Otherwise he would never touch you.

With my benefit money I could afford to take the bus to see Mama and Jim. They had moved from Blackwood to a cottage in the countryside. The time I spent there with them, Lydia and her partner Craig, a kind and gentle Englishman who made beautiful art and even better jokes, was the best escape I could hope for. They loved me through everything. I didn't want to live but I didn't quite want to die either. They accepted me as a ghost, perhaps friendly like Casper I'm not quite sure, that floated around the cottage and sometimes zoned out of conversations. They noticed my brain fog and mental lapses but were patient with me. The most upsetting thing about my concentration failing was that I found it difficult to read books. Another piece of the world was lost to me as those once upright letters crumbled.

My old friend Imogen from Glasgow wrote to me. She still lived in the West End so when I had enough money for train fare and was able to stand the crush of grumpy passengers, I visited her. She was incredibly kind to me. In the lemon light of her bathroom she'd run me baths and pour in soaping heaps of fancy bubble bath. She would take me to Kelvingrove Park and peel off my socks and lay my feet gently in the grass, occasionally tickling them with a green leaf.

We laughed and ate cake in bed. She booked us a night at the Hilton and we giggled at being served like we were fancy ladies. Our mouths went numb from the gin-laced sorbet. We slid across the glossy foyer hall and took a taxi to the theatre. From the gallery I watched the light from the stage illuminate Imogen's face. She was so beautiful. After the show we headed to a salsa club in the square. Our faces painted with flowers, we watched as the dancers wrapped themselves around each other. The women moved like liquid magenta. We fell asleep in our dresses and face paint. Imogen threaded her fingers through mine and we stayed like that till morning.

What I felt for Imogen was stronger than friendship. It was unspoken on my end but she knew it. The one time we crossed that particular line we were both too drunk and it didn't feel right. I wasn't connected to my body. Not in that way. Pleasure eluded me. I was like those pickled aliens from shows in the 60s, a blob of grey matter suspended in a laboratory beaker. In another time and another place who knows what Imogen and I might have been to each other. But it wasn't this life.

On St Patrick's Day Imogen persuaded me to go drinking with her and her friends. It had been a few months since I'd been out. We headed to a club where the floor was sticky and the drinks were cheap. It was exactly the same as it always was but I had changed. With a dead expression I stood at the bar and watched as people were sick in corners.

On my way to find Imogen through the crowd I felt a hand on my skirt and another pulling at my wrist. I ripped my arm away, not caring if I dislocated their shoulder in the process. I couldn't stand being touched. Being pawed at like a piece of meat. Rage bloomed in my chest and I wanted to scream and tear the people around me. I stared at the crowd with revulsion and wanted to spew acid on their faces. I wanted to hurt them – to show them that I was done. That I was tired of being pulled apart and hastily stitched back together. That after years of it, the cuts were uneven and parts were still missing.

That was the last night I ever went to a club.

White Room

I promised Mama and Lydia that I would book an appointment with the doctor.

The months were slipping past with no improvement. It was as if I were floating in stagnant marsh water. Terrified I would be laughed out of the GP office I sat in the waiting room and tried to avoid making eye contact with any other patients. A little girl played near my feet with a toy horse.

The GP was harried and short on time so we skipped through a checklist for depression and five minutes later I was at the pharmacy with a prescription for Prozac.

Mama was unhappy. "Did you tell them everything?"

"Yes, Mama I told them everything."

A lie.

Of course I hadn't. If I told them about the thoughts then the thoughts would happen. That was my screwed-up logic. I had come to know irrationality intimately. Prozac did little to change my obsessions but instead amplified the garish colours of my nightmares. I was too nervous to go back to the doctor and so I kept taking the pills.

The following week there was a Blackwood reunion with some of my old school friends and on the train I applied my lipstick and practised smiling in the mirror. My friends and I tried to sketch each other a picture of our lives over the past few years, something that carried the colours of that time, but the colours seemed muted. I slipped into the bathroom and took my Prozac with my wine. I texted a friend to pick up another bottle or two.

The alcohol wasn't working like it used to.

More of my friends arrived and the room hummed with music and laughter. I sat beside the open patio door. The sky loomed above and I felt drawn to the violet ether.

But something burned.

On my left side there was a growing ache. There was a dull roar, a rush in my head and I tipped forward and threw up over the patio. My friends carried me to the bathroom and I lay over the cool ceramic of the tub.

"I don't understand. I never throw up," I said.

It had been a bizarre point of pride. I could drink however much I wanted and never get sick.

In the bathroom I threw up again and this time it was blended with dark blood. Granules like congealed coffee stuck to bottom of the tub. The pain grew sharper and my friends called Lydia. When she arrived, she morphed from her tiny five-foot-one frame and somehow picked me up from the floor. She swaddled me in an old jumper and told me I was safe.

Back at the flat, the pain of the knife in my side meant I couldn't lie down or sit up so I kept to a halfway position while episodes of Mad Men played in the background. It seemed like a strange trick of fate that they should be ones where Don Draper was blacking out and sitting on his freezing porch trying to sober up.

The universe certainly has a sense of humour.

66

Around the twenty-fifth time I threw up everything grew fuzzy. The television blared downstairs. Dad was watching some comedy compilation from the 1970s when I managed to make it downstairs.

"Something's not right," I said.

"You just went a bit overboard last night. We've all been there. You just need to sleep it off," he said, barely taking his eyes off the screen.

As I padded out of the living room I could hear him laughing at the show. Growing nervous I tried to replace the fluids I was losing but the sips of water didn't stay in my system for very long. Then the shaking started. I called on Dad but there was no answer. My body didn't stop jerking so finally I screamed and after a few minutes the door opened.

"Something's really not right."

Dad looked at me with one eyebrow raised, unconvinced, and pulled me down to the kitchen to get water. "You just need to drink something." I gave up and lay on the kitchen floor and begged for his phone to call NHS 24. A gentle lady came on the line. My abdomen grew cold. After a few minutes she said, "Listen we're going to send an ambulance round to get you, okay. We won't be too long so don't fret. Try to get a wee blanket over you and keep on your side for me okay, darling?"

"Thank you so much."

Dad came back in the room and folded his arms.

"So did they just say the same? Fluids and rest?"

"D-dad they are sending an ambulance," I said between shakes.

He was silent for a moment.

"Well that's good then I suppose," he said and shrugged. "Best to get it checked for your peace of mind and then you can come back and sleep it off."

Two paramedics arrived and picked me up using a blanket. Dad hovered unsure in the background and then followed as they took me into the ambulance and tried to find a vein.

"Sorry pet, you must feel like a pincushion."

They weren't able to find a vein so when we arrived at the hospital the doctors in emergency care took over. Two different doctors tried until a nurse found one. She eyed my arms and shook her head. "What have they done to you?"

Mama's anxious face edged into view. Her eyes were bright with tears. She wiped the sweat off my face and nervously eyed the sick bowl which was thick with dark pieces. A familiar bird-like woman wandered past my door and immediately backtracked, her mouth slightly agape. When I locked eyes with her, she fixed her expression into a smile.

"Bit weird you're hanging out in a hospital!" Lydia joked.

I grimaced and her face grew serious. "Really though, how are you doing?"

"Been better."

Her eyes didn't meet mine.

"You know I walked right past you. I thought, who's that poor soul? Looks like they've overdosed on drugs," she said and fidgeted with the sleeve of her cardigan. "But it was you."

They wheeled me from the Emergency Room to the Surgical Ward. Mama, Lydia and Dad all pattered down the corridor behind me.

"But I'm just saying there's ways to go about things!" Lydia hissed, her face growing red.

Dad bit back, "I'm just trying here."

"Yes. Maybe try a different way." Lydia held up a leaflet and jabbed it with a finger. "This? This is not the way to go about things."

There was one word, larger than the rest, printed in the middle that I managed to make out.

Suicide.

But I wasn't trying to kill myself.

I fell asleep and woke to an alien planet subsumed in green LED light with beeping noises and the whirring of the IV. There was a glow coming from down the hallway at the nurses' station. They had ordered food for the night shift. The greasy smell of takeaway wafted down the corridor and my stomach lurched but I didn't throw up. Those anti-emetics were really something. I was terribly thirsty. The kind of thirst I imagined vampires must have, a dry itch at the back of their throat that was never quite quenched. They wheeled me down the corridor for an ultrasound. A television flickered in the corner of the room and I thought about St Michaels and Greta and her little tuft of hair.

The doctor told me that I had acute pancreatitis. This basically meant that because of the amount of alcohol in my system my pancreas got the wrong signal and released huge amounts of digestive enzymes. The enzymes then started to digest my own pancreas. The doctor explained I was lucky and that there were many patients with acute pancreatitis where their pancreas necrotises and digests itself to the point of the flesh dying.

"You realise how serious this is? You could have died, yes?"

I stared at my bedsheets.

Then he asked me a question I was not prepared for.

"Now do you need any help getting off it? The alcohol?"

I shook my head and he nodded curtly and left the room. Dad arrived looking around the ward blankly.

"Got your text. Had a Google. There's a guy at work whose mum had it."

"Is she okay?"

Dad stared around at the other patients, "Hm – what? Oh yes, she's fine. Healed up and back to normal now."

"The doctor said something about help getting off it." I fidgeted with the blue NHS blanket.

Dad laughed. "Oh no! No, it's different than they say online. Like I said that guy's mum is just fine. You can still drink. Just the minimum per week. So that's what, around fourteen units? That's two bottles of wine. Obviously give it a couple of months but you'll be back to normal in no time."

Dad made it sound ridiculous.

I reasoned that the doctor mistook me for someone else who got this kind of disease – some kind of chronic drinker who ended up in the hospital every few months. I cottoned onto Dad's line of thinking.

"Maybe if I'd eaten something I wouldn't have been quite so ill? Or not drank as much?"

"Just bad luck," Dad said and shrugged.

But it wasn't bad luck. I had poisoned myself. My substance abuse was symptomatic of a deeper pain. I was attempting to cauterise my own psychic wounds with the only solution I thought I had available to me. I was wrong of course. But I couldn't have known that back then. I was still in denial. And so I listened to my dad.

Mama barrelled through the door and before I knew it I was in the familiar powdery smell of her scarf. "I brought you this," she said and fished out a bottle of diluting juice she had made. "Water from the cottage. It'll heal you in no time."

I took a grateful sip.

A wave of weariness came over me so I closed my eyes as Mama and Dad sat on opposite ends of my bed. There was a gnawing guilt because I knew it was my fault they had to be in the same room. Drifting in and out of restless waves I noticed Mama's eyes steeled and her arms folded around herself. They attempted small talk but her voice was clipped as if she wished to give him no more than she would politely give a stranger on the street.

After two days I was discharged from the hospital. My arms and legs were mottled blue and I had a gash on my right arm from the IV. Lydia had packed me clothes. A beautiful mint green dress. I couldn't help but laugh at such a ridiculous going home outfit although the mint did accentuate the green tinge of my skin rather nicely.

Dad took time off work but I found myself wondering who it was really for. He didn't pay much attention to me and mostly played poker on his phone. On the third night I made a grave mistake in choosing something hot for dinner rather than the yoghurts I'd been living on. The single bite of food laboured down my oesophagus and I found myself wishing I could claw it back out from my throat. It was too late and I had the acute joy of being able to feel every inch of the food pass down, roasting the already seared flesh. I read about oesophageal holes online and wondered how I could have been so stupid.

Dad went back to work and I was alone again. But there was a little piece of happiness – I was allowed to take my first bath. The warmth radiated to the centre of my bones and the pain blurred at the edges. I dried off in a fluffy blue towel and was careful to pat the gash from the IV gently. Perhaps it was a small omen of what was to come because as I patted it dry I noticed that the wound was stitching itself up.

Red Jumper

There is a strange illogical nature to obsessions. The obsessive mind is like that of a crypt full of shadows and skeletons. Your greatest fears are recited like hallowed verse from a holy text and yet even as they penetrate the whorls of your brain – they never get it quite right. Something goes missing in the translation.

It would still be a few years before I realised one small but powerful fact – perhaps one of the most important to my recovery – that the content of my obsessions was not the problem. The trauma they contained was survivable. More than liveable. Instead, it was the threat never fully realised. The dark apparition of a future that would never come to be. The blade in the shadow. That was the truly destructive thing. Obsessions had little to do with reality and I would soon come to realise this when pain and death came to my family.

My granda.

Granda loved clocks. I'm not sure why. Perhaps in a universe that often felt unknowable – one that could turn on a whim – the steady tick of time was the only constant, reliable thing.

Or maybe he just liked clocks.

There were at least twelve in the living room alone. When daylight savings kicked in it would take all day to change each clock in the house to the right time. Still, some would be just a fraction off leading to a slightly discordant ticking noise. I liked that sound. Maybe my brain worked on the same frequency. Mostly I think it was because that was the sound of Granda's living room.

When I visited, he would always show me the same photograph of my gran. We lost her when I was fifteen. I loved her. My gran understood. She knew I wasn't well. When I woke screaming from nightmares, she held me and told me she knew how to quiet the terrors because she'd been a nurse and worked in a mental hospital.

As a child I got to stay up late at Gran and Granda's house. Buttoned up in my pyjamas, I cuddled beside them and watched Law and Order while drinking hot chocolate. Moments with my family often quelled the tide of disquiet I usually felt. For a while I felt safe. There was a steadiness to Granda's house like it existed outside of the loop of time. Like it would always be.

But we lost Gran and five years later Granda was diagnosed with cancer.

From Hamilton I took the bus and train to the house full of clocks on Kinnelar Drive. When I visited, I gave Granda the tightest hug and accidentally knocked his glasses askew. He was wearing his favourite red jumper.

"He isn't defiant in the way I imagined he would be," Lydia said to me in the kitchen as we made tea. "He's quiet."

Granda began radiotherapy but it made him feel so unwell that after speaking with the doctor they decided not to continue treatment. He shrunk in his red jumper and didn't have much of an appetite.

Lydia and I spent a quiet Christmas at the cottage. We woke at 6am to cows bellowing and ended up laughing so much we couldn't get back to sleep. Before lunch we went for a walk along the country lanes. The air was like glass, the shards catching in my throat. At night I tried to sleep but I couldn't stop thinking about Granda.

When I woke up on Boxing Day morning I knew something was wrong.

The car journey was difficult. Lydia was to pick up Dad at his girlfriend's house before driving us all over to our uncle's where Granda and the whole family would be swapping presents in a mad flurry of wrapping paper and ribbons. I was anxious before even arriving. In the car thoughts of Lydia hurtling into the dashboard punctured my mind. I tried to focus on my breathing but it didn't work. The anxiety built in sharp waves and in the back of the car I had to run my hands over my eyes and underwear to check.

I pictured Granda waiting at the house for us. I saw his pained expression as he tried to suppress the pain of the disease tearing at his insides.

I can't let him down, I thought.

Dad was exuberant. He had always loved Boxing Day. Not because he got to see his own dad, Granda, or the rest of the family. No, for him it was little more than an excuse to drink all day. Dad told Lydia and I to come inside and say hello. Apparently his girlfriend and all her family were gathered inside. I had never met them before. They were strangers to me.

I found myself rooted to my seat.

"I can't."

Dad's face twisted.

"What do you mean you can't?" he hissed through gritted teeth. "You're being very rude. All I'm asking for is five minutes here."

"I can't do it. Please. Let me stay here."

"Yes you can, get your stuff and let's go. Come on. It'll be five minutes."

Lydia looked concerned.

"Maybe she can just stay here?"

Dad sat back and let out an exasperated sigh.

"Look it's Boxing Day and I'm just asking for this one thing." He shot a look at me cowering in the back. "Fine. Never mind. Come on, Lydia. You stay here, Jillian."

He slammed the door and it reverberated in my skull.

In the back of the car a memory came back to me.

I was eight years old again.

"I won't be too long!" Dad called as he slammed the car door.

I was eight years old and Dad was going to get us a takeaway. It was mid-winter and my breath billowed from my mouth in thick clouds.

He'll be back soon, I thought.

I turned on some music. Fifteen minutes turned into thirty which turned to an hour. I flicked through all the radio stations faster and faster until the static fuzzed over and made me feel sick. I switched the radio off.

Red.

He's not coming back.

No, that's stupid, I thought. Of course he is.

He's been hurt and he isn't coming back. And no one knows you are here. No one will find you. And if they do, can you imagine what they'll do with you? They're going to hurt you. Very badly. So maybe it's better if you aren't found after all.

I put my hands under my knees to keep them warm.

You'll probably freeze and die in here.

Stop it, I thought.

He's dead. And you won't make it.

STOP IT.

Rocking back and forth I covered my ears and prayed I would stop crying. In the rearview mirror I tried to catch a glimpse of him but the street was empty. I made myself small so no one passing by could see me. So they couldn't hurt me. I stayed like that for a long time. The door opened and I freaked out thinking it was a bad man. But it was Dad. He was back. He was alive. I gave him a feeble smile but noticed a familiar scent.

"Sorry about that! Food took a bit longer so decided to get a pint while I was waiting," he said.

He didn't notice my tear-stained face. He just passed me a bag of takeaway food. It sat on my lap, cold and congealing, the entire drive home.

A dull static roar brought me back to Boxing Day.

With my nerves flayed I checked the streets around me. A figure approached the car and I was convinced they were going to open the door and hurt me. But it was just Dad and Lydia.

"Are you okay, darling?" Lydia said.

Words left me. There was no shape or meaning to them. Nothing that could describe the black static in my mind. Dad eyed me in the mirror. A shadow of anger passed in his expression. I was ruining his Boxing Day.

The black static grew and the visible outlines of Lydia and Dad began to fail. The only clear thing was Granda sitting in the house, looking at the window, in his red jumper. Then he left me.

The car stopped and Lydia asked if I wanted to go inside my uncle's house where Granda and the rest of the family were gathered.

"Of course she's going inside!" Dad spat.

"Give her a minute will you?" says Lydia.

I sat motionless in the back seat, the green hood of my parka over my face.

"This has gone on for far too long. Come on, Jillian do your breathing and you'll be fine. Wipe your face. Come on now."

"No," I said softly.

Dad threw up his hands. "I'm clearly not accomplishing anything here so I'm going inside."

After he left I heard Lydia's voice, soft like a chime, "What do you want me to do, darling?"

I could make out her voice at the end of the tunnel. I tried to get to her.

"It's okay, pea, it's okay, you don't need to pull." I didn't realise I was grasping at her desperately.

"Help... please..."

"Okay, darling, that's what we're going to do. I'm going to call Mama, okay. I'll give you a moment alone but I'll just be making the call beside the car. I won't be far. We're going to help you, darling."

The black static spiked in my ears. Everything light was lost. Everyone would get sick. Everyone would die. There was only pain left. In the back seat of the car, I was so scared but mostly I was tired of living with that acidic fear. I knew what would finally stop it. The soft release of opening the door and stepping into traffic. It would be over quickly. Just a few steps and then it would be quiet. I was ready for it to end now. I pulled down the door handle but it was locked.

Lydia came back to the car and handed me her phone. Mama's voice came over the line. A brilliant light pierced its way through the dark. She asked if I needed to go to the hospital. I said yes. While Lydia was inside telling Dad, I tried the door handle but she'd locked it again. Any fight left me and the tide pulled me under. On the way to the hospital, I was vaguely aware of Lydia speaking gently to me but she might as well have been light years away.

At A&E, Lydia spoke with a nurse who kindly put me in a side area away from the crowd of people. The metallic smell of blood inflamed my nose. I tried to stop my mind picturing what lay on the other side of the curtain. Head injuries, people with objects impaled in their body, a paper cup cellotaped over a damaged eye.

I kept the hood of my parka up.

The doctor asked me if I was a danger to myself or others. She asked me if I thought I might hurt myself. I knew where they would take me if I said yes. At St Michaels I had been on the other side. For a moment I wondered if that might be the right thing. If I said yes, I could sleep in a clean bed with hospital staff around. Maybe they would put me on a medication that would stop the obsessions. But I was scared to be alone. Lydia's face was the only thing that made sense to me. I told the doctor I wouldn't hurt myself, that I was just tired. She raised her eyebrow and told me they didn't want to send me away when there was a bed here, but I shook my head and she sent me home with Diazepam and an urgent referral for psychiatric services.

The blue winter dusk enveloped us as we walked down the lane to the car. Lydia found a sweet in her pocket and joked about wanting to trade for my medication. I would never be able to tell my sister how grateful I was. Her love made living bearable. The medication subsumed the black static and I grew sleepy. As we walked I peered a little more closely at the hospital buildings and in some uncertain way they seemed familiar to me.

"Where are we, Lydia?"

"The Western Infirmary, darling."

We were in the West End. From behind the trees I noticed the Glasgow University building next to the hospital. Somewhere down the hill was my old dormitory.

The following fortnight I spent time at the cottage recovering from the Boxing Day breakdown.

Every morning I took my medication just like the doctor prescribed. Mama smoothed my hair and tucked me into bed. Jim made me cups of green tea and said he was around if I needed to talk. I wanted to cry. I didn't feel like I deserved their love.

The winter air was still with shades of lavender as I walked the dogs. It was my first time outside in a while. The dogs gambled around, sniffing frosted leaves and squaring off against rogue sheep by the fence.

Something gnawed at me.

Dad didn't come with us to the hospital. Instead he had a beer in the front room. After all, it was his Boxing Day. There was the rage again. Untethered in my chest. It sparked until it was replaced by the same guilt I felt as a child at thinking badly of him. Narcissists are very good at having an explanation for everything, for making you doubt yourself. And my dad was no exception. I thought no matter what he did, he'd always get away with it. I didn't realise at the time that there was a way out.

But for now there were more important things going on.

Granda was moved to St Margaret of Scotland Hospice. The building was bright and clean and there was a gentle air to the place that the staff worked tirelessly to cultivate and protect. In Granda's room the nurses created a little home around his bedside. The care staff seemed to almost float down the hallways. Their faces were always lined with a kind expression. I didn't know how they managed to bear what they saw but there was an unknowable strength that radiated from them. A silver aura that looped around their whole body.

Lydia whispered, "They aren't from this world. I just know it."

Though he joked with the nurses, Granda wasn't happy at the hospice and so we moved him home. None of us were prepared for the slow violence of the disease. Granda shrunk to a small shape under the white covers. Lydia was at his bedside every day. She worked beside him, pausing to talk or adjust his pillow. She helped him drink his milk. Granda drifted in and out of sleep, but Lydia was there for him in his conscious moments.

Granda was happier to be home. In his own room with his family close by. Sometimes it shames me to say this, but the truth was I wanted him to be free. Free from the pain and the disease that held him in its vice like grip. I didn't want him to leave us, but I didn't want him to have to live like this anymore.

Soon the twilight moments were all that were left to us.

Granda was made comfortable. He wasn't in any more pain. Like the Western films he loved I imagined him walking through an impossible dessert, his legs unsteady as he trekked through the burnt-orange earth searching for the grove. I prayed for my Gran to come and take him. To walk hand and hand, just like they had always done, from this world to another.

Lydia was with him in his last moments. He took his last breath and left the world a little less bright.

After his death I drifted in and out of sleep. In my dream I was at Kinnelar Drive. The clocks ticked quietly and Gran and Granda were sitting happily on their matching armchairs. Granda was eating a roll with little crumbs resting on his jumper. He winked at me over his paper.

I don't understand, how can you be here? I thought.

Gran laughed, her eyes twinkling, "Silly Jillian. We never went anywhere in the first place. We were always here."

For a moment on that sunny afternoon there was a reprieve. There was still love to be found on that sad day. My heart ached but I also felt such relief. Granda was free from pain. He was with Gran. Sometimes it was as if the next world over made more sense than this one.

In the afternoon I woke from my nap and didn't perform my compulsions. I padded down the stairs feeling a small bit of hope. Like I said before, the universe turns in ways you could never understand. I didn't know it yet but at the bottom of the stairs I would come across the thing that set me down a path of recovery. The very thing that would lead me to my diagnosis, my sobriety and a real chance at life.

There was an eviction letter at the door.

Daylight Flit

Final Notice.

Eviction.

Dad hadn't been paying the rent. He hadn't even bothered to open the countless envelopes warning him to pay the arrears or call and speak to someone. He ignored them. He ignored them because, using his logic, a problem didn't exist if you ignored it.

Maybe that's why he ignored me.

But I wasn't a problem. I was his daughter. I suppose that still wasn't enough.

When I saw the eviction letter I spiralled into panic but part of me wasn't surprised. In twenty-one years Dad had never been the kind of person you could depend on, so why did I expect it now? He would always put himself, his drink, his gambling and his glib sense of happiness first. I was so sick that I thought maybe this time he would pull through, but I had been wrong and now it was time to get out while I had a chance. Before he got his hooks back into me and I spent the rest of my life tethered to him.

The following day I went to Citizens Advice. A soft-spoken lady brought me into her office and I explained everything. My nose grew pink as a mouse as I tried not to cry. The lady said simply, "Right then. Let's get everything sorted for you."

She handed me a tissue that smelled faintly of lavender and I blew gratefully into it.

In these kinds of places – Citizens Advice, the Job Centre, the doctor's surgery and hospital – I had always been blessed with tired looking men and women who fought for me. There were so many points along the road that things could have turned out very differently but these people saved me. It's because of them that I had a chance.

The soft-spoken lady placed me on a list for emergency housing and in the meantime told me to look for flats that housing benefits would cover. Before I left she looked at me and told me everything was going to be okay.

And I believed her.

After a few days of searching I found a flat and made an appointment with the letting agency. By this time I had told Mama everything and she drove over and took me to the cottage. The next day we visited the new flat. I dressed in the only formal piece of clothing I had left. A white shirt with a button missing. I fixed this by wearing a black cardigan over it. The cardigan's sleeve had come undone at the wrist but if I kept it clasped together in my hand you couldn't really tell.

After the flat viewing, Mama told me she and Lydia had the deposit ready to go. I shouldn't have been surprised. They had always been there.

It shamed me to give them so little in return.

That night I lit a candle and rubbed my fingers along the base of my skull. I was terrified of sharp objects. They seemed to possess a life of their own and I was convinced I would lose control and stab myself. But that night I held a pair of scissors in my hand. Purpose trumped fear. I grabbed a lock of hair from the base of my neck and sawed through it with the blunt craft scissors. I placed the lock of hair next to the burning candle and prayed. Please let me leave this place, I thought.

I promised myself that if I got the flat it would be the start of a new chapter. And that when I was able to pay Mama and Lydia back it wouldn't just be with the money. I knew that once I was able to get away from Dad that I might have a chance.

The next day I got a phone call telling me the flat was mine.

The week before I moved Mama took me out to the garden at the cottage. She wrapped me up in her old coat and shoved a purple hat on my head so I looked like a gloomy thistle pitching back and forth in the garden.

"Just a few things to clear before Spring starts, my darling," she said.

She grasped at the necks of plants as if they were her patients to diagnose and forced an unfamiliar metal object into my hands. Its cool weight burned my hand and I dropped it.

I also hated metal tools. I hated their cool violence. Even at rest they seemed threatening. Knives were the worst but hammers were a close second. They played the part of a useful tool and yet I could only think of how many serial killers have carried them. After all, who would second guess a hammer stashed in a toolbox? But a hammer could quickly turn into a tool of violence. Even in their inert state I felt that threat. And it terrified me.

Mama picked up the clippers and told me I was okay. She said we were going to deadhead each of the flowers in turn. Deadheading was a process of pruning fading flowers. With the metal clippers in my hand I had to stop myself from tearing my nails off to expose the fleshy bed underneath. After a while the thoughts retreated and as I clipped each flower I felt a similar dead growth cast off from me.

Dusk fell upon us and we retreated to the kitchen for coffee and tea and biscuits. There was a smudge of dirt on my cheek and though the circuits of my brain were a little frazzled I had the feeling I'd overcome something even if it was only the smallest of victory.

Mama put down her coffee and looked at me. "Now this might sound strange but it's important that you don't tell your dad about moving out."

Part of me didn't understand until I saw the anxiety that lined Mama's face. She had never wanted me at his in the first place but respected my autonomy. Years later I'd ask her and she'd tell me she wanted to get in the car every night and come get me. We all thought it would be temporary but as the days went on she grew sicker – not knowing how to get me out while still considering my own volition. She just had to hope the day would come where I could find enough mental strength and clarity to pull myself out.

That day had come.

I knew what she was saying. Dad wouldn't let me go. He'd start to talk just like he always did and soon convince me I wasn't well enough, that I was sick and should stay with him.

That he would look after me.

That it would all be different.

No. It had to be a secret. Otherwise there'd be no chance of getting out.

At the kitchen table I turned to Mama and asked, "Am I well enough?"

She looked out the window and said, "I think you'll be a whole lot better once you get out of there."

So Mama and I attempted a daylight flit. It wasn't in the cover of night and it wasn't to escape unpaid debts. It was to get away from him. The week before I moved I quietly packed all my things into boxes. I didn't need many. Years of moving had accustomed me to leaving things behind. Dad didn't notice anyway. His daughter packed up her whole life and he didn't suspect a thing. Eviction loomed closer and my stomach twisted every morning when the door was banged by people Dad owed money to. History repeats itself. I was just like Mama after the divorce trying to escape.

On the morning of the daylight flit, Mama arrived in her car and I rushed up and down the stairs loading the car with battered boxes. The smoke from her cigarette clouded Mama in an anxious haze. She kept eyeing the rearview mirror. As I squashed the last stuffed animal into the car she snuffed out her cigarette. Mama pushed back her sunglasses and I could see her steeled gaze, resolute.

"Time to say goodbye, darling."

From the front seat I looked up at my bedroom window with its broken blind. The outside with its peeling paint. Part of me felt sad for this neglected home. The bones of it were there for me and provided shelter and hot baths and a place to rest. But the psychic energy in that house was toxic and I grew weary living with a vampire. Still, I looked at my old room and whispered under my breath, "Thank you for keeping me safe."

With one last anxious look in the rearview mirror, Mama floored it and we sped into the unknowable horizon.

Carluke

Strange trails led me to Carluke.

Mama and I flipped over a cardboard box and set out our lunch as a little picnic. I couldn't believe how quiet it was. The only noise was from a few birds chirping outside on the mossy ledge. Their burnished beaks cheeped open as if they were welcoming me.

Mama sat eating a sandwich. "Well isn't this just lovely?"

She checked my boiler, water and heating and made sure there was enough electricity in the meter. She filled the fridge with fresh fruit, sandwiches and chocolate and left floral dish towels by the sink.

"I'll be over in a minute if you need me, but I know you're going to thrive here, darling," she said and patted my head as if I were a seedling trying to take hold in fresh dirt.

After she left I tiptoed around the flat hardly believing it to be real. My mind was half-convinced it was only temporary like a special hotel visit and that I'd be back at Dad's tomorrow.

But it wasn't.

It was real and it was mine.

Before I settled for the night I had to make a call.

"Hello?" Dad's voice crackled through the static. My stomach lurched and I closed my eyes in case somehow he could see me.

"Is that you, Jillian?"

"Yes. It's me. Everything is okay." I pressed my eyes tighter, took a deep breath and spluttered, "Everything is okay. But the thing is, I don't really know how to say this – but I wanted you to know before you got back to the flat – because – well – I don't live there anymore."

"Excuse me?"

"I got a flat, Dad. I found it online. I'm here now. I'm safe. I'm grateful for you letting me stay but it was time –"

"You moved out?"

"Yes."

"Today?"

"Yes."

"And I suppose your Mum helped you?"

"Yes."

There was a beat of silence.

"Well I can't say I'm not concerned. Had I known about this I would have said no if I'm being quite honest. You aren't exactly in a fit state to be living alone. You're still very unwell."

"I know."

"So why did you go? And why didn't you tell me?"

With a sigh I sat down in the corner of the room and burrowed into the wall. "I found the letter."

"What letter?"

"I know you aren't supposed to look at other people's mail but I saw eviction on it and I panicked and went to the housing office and they helped me."

There was laughter on his end of the line. "Oh you don't need to worry about that. I've sorted it. I've called them and

88

we've set up a plan. I'll pay some rent now and then stick to the payment plan. You see?"

"Oh."

"Yes, see you would have known this if you'd spoken to me. This is all very strange."

"Yes. I was just... scared."

"Even more reason. It seems frankly bizarre to have you out there on your own." I heard him pause before he tried to sound casual. "Where even are you?"

"Carluke."

I froze and wondered if I should have given him the name.

"You send me the address and I'll come see you. This all seems frankly bizarre, Jillian."

"I'm sorry. I didn't know what to do."

"Well," he clicked his tongue.

The line went dead.

Through my nausea something cast off me just like when I was deadheading the flowers. Another shadow that had been around for so long I'd been unable to recognise its shape or name. My body, which a minute before had been wracked with tension, suddenly relaxed. I stopped trying to burrow into the wall and instead walked into the centre of the room. I stretched out my limbs and made myself as big as I could, my fingertips to the ceiling and my toes on the soft carpet.

A newfound excitement stirred in me and I jumped around a few times and sang the words of a silly pop song.

That night as I lay in bed even the birds were quiet.

It was as if I was in some kind of bizarre witness protection programme. No one knew me in Carluke and yet I didn't feel like a stranger in the town. The bathroom mirror reflected a freckled face. My eyes were lighter and I had dyed my hair back to its original ginger colour. With iron ore and copper, I tried to rebuild myself. Skipping out in blue jean shorts, an oversized

89

jumper and hemp shoes, I smelled the turn of the season. The wildflowers were back.

There was an interlude to the thoughts of violence as I walked through the countryside. There was a communion with nature that I had been missing. Rainbow coloured halos formed in my vision as I stared just a little too long at the sky. I wondered if it had always been so open.

On my walks the great trees that lined the streets pulled me in, broad and strong, their limbs embracing me. I'd put my hand on their trunks and feel myself being grounded and circled in their ancient protection. A little spark of my spirituality and my hippy pagan childhood that brought me such joy was igniting within me again and it felt wonderful.

Returning home with flushed cheeks and damp hair on my neck, I made tea and settled myself on my little sofa bed with its broken springs. To save money I was careful not to turn on the storage radiator or the boiler, instead using a small electric heater to warm up the room. Pulling on knitted socks I'd heat my toes up on the little orange patch of heat reflected on the carpet and try to hold myself still in the moment.

How sweet the interlude could be.

This small town gifted me separation from Dad and the space to get better. When I first arrived the flat was like a second womb where I could try to heal. If only I'd known then how insidious this disease is. New obsessions would soon latch on and new compulsions would threaten to break my sanity. But at this time in my life I still didn't know what I was fighting. Even though the disorder was about to evolve in ways I could have never imagined – my diagnosis would be the key to understanding it all.

There was still hope to be found – in the form of three letters.

OCD

I had grown used to the sharp smell of antiseptic when the hospital doors opened. I had grown used to kind receptionists and battered waiting room chairs. Of nodding meekly to other patients across the aisle. Of wondering how they found themselves there that day. A figure in a white coat drew into focus. She smiled gently and we walked along another long corridor together. She told me to make myself comfortable. Only her face was in focus. The white edges of her coat blurred.

She asked me to tell her about my thoughts. My mind was caged in dark spaces, places of blood. I closed my eyes and shook my head.

"I can't say them out loud."

"And why's that?"

"Because if I say them out loud they will happen."

"It's okay. I know how scary this must be. I understand if you're not ready but I'd really love to be able to help you and the only way I'm going to be able to do that is if you tell me what kind of thoughts you've been having."

Red.

"Please…"

The doctor sat beside me.

"You're safe here. It's very important you say out loud what is happening when you have these thoughts. I know you feel like you can't but I promise nothing bad is going to happen to you if you do."

Her face was gentle and I could see little shadows under her eyes. I wondered how long her shift was. I took a deep breath. And told her everything.

Blood. Eyes. Limbs. Broken. Skulls. Torn. Flesh. Vagina. Rip.

Knives.

The doctor nodded as I detailed my thoughts of decapitated children and nails and hammers. She didn't flinch and back away from me as if I were monster. She didn't look at me like I was crazy when I told her I could feel the violent things happening in my body. That each thought was accompanied by a sharp burst of residual pain.

The doctor went back to her desk and wrote something down on a yellow pad. After a moment or two she lifted her head and said, "Jillian from everything you've told me here today it's very clear that you have Obsessive Compulsive Disorder."

And there it was. A twin melody of relief and sadness flowed through me. The madness had a name but that also meant it was real. There was no reinvention of myself I could make. No relocation to a different city. No new group of friends. No new university course. No new outfit or haircut or bottle of wine that would fix me.

But it had a name.

And I could work to understand it. I could learn how it worked and maybe even how to treat it.

"The best course of action for OCD is a round of anti-depressants alongside therapy. The medication will get you stable enough to do the work required in therapy," the doctor said before hesitating. "It's not going to be easy. OCD is incurable but it can be managed and there is hope for many who are compliant with treatment."

Hope is more than something, I thought.

She wished me luck and I floated along the hospital corridor in a daze. Mama and I sat in the car together and I showed her the bright yellow sheet of paper with my diagnosis on it. She hugged me and said everything was going to be okay. I could feel her tears, wet on my head. She kissed me and told me she was proud of me.

We drove from the hospital through winding country lanes. The sun filtered through the overcast sky and I let myself cry. Through my tears I found myself breaking into a smile before crying again. There was a strange swell of emotions in my chest. Anxiety and sadness. A little grief and loss.

But the overwhelming feeling was one of relief.

Mama stole glances at me from the driver's seat. We had been fighting off demons in the dark but my diagnosis had gifted us the steel to fight and possibly win.

Hope is more than something.

OCD like many other mental disorders is still not entirely understood. It is difficult to parse the eddies of the mind and the chemical and cognitive functions that we are prey to.

But we do know some things.

OCD is a chronic condition with often lifelong morbidity.

OCD is polygenic and among the factors that work to trigger the disorder – genetics and environmental are most often cited.

Obsessions and compulsions work in tandem with one other and in turn strengthen the feedback of the loop.

There are different 'themes' of OCD and after my diagnosis I read up on them all.

With Contamination OCD, people might wash their hands until they bleed. They can develop chest problems from the inhalation of bleach fumes while cleaning or scald their bodies in boiling water in the shower because they never feel clean enough. Their families can become reduced in their mind to vectors carrying germs. For some, touch is something that is no longer permitted in their life.

Scrupulosity or Religious or Moral OCD is where the person's obsessions are centred on the fear that they have acted in an immoral or sinful way. They experience intense guilt and spiritual anguish and can often feel they deserve to be punished for disobeying their higher power. They can obsess over yelling out blasphemous statements in church and often pray excessively to alleviate their guilt.

Unwanted sexual thoughts is another form of OCD where the person can experience distressing obsessions surrounding incest, paedophilia or other intrusive sexual thoughts. Sufferers often check themselves for signs of sexual arousal when the obsessions occur. Their fear itself can trigger an arousal response and make them believe they are what they fear themselves to be. When masturbating intrusive thoughts can pop into their mind at the time of climax and they can see this as proof they are sexually deviant in some way.

With Harm OCD, those suffering have aggressive and violent obsessions and a fear of hurting people around them. Their thoughts might be centred on smashing a baby against a wall or of hurting innocent children in a playground or stabbing their father.

Sounded familiar.

I came to understand Harm OCD as a major theme of my own OCD. The only difference for me was the theme was often inverted. A lot of my obsessions centred on harm coming to me and my family from the violent actions of other people. And very often I was afraid of my own body turning on me.

Regardless of theme OCD sufferers turn on themselves, often engaging in self harm. Suicide numbers are high. Obsessive compulsive disorder is insidious, slowly draining life and meaning from a person and making them live in fear until death seems like a quieter, kinder option.

After my diagnosis I received a letter for a work assessment interview. The nurse conducting my interview was incredibly patient. She asked about the nature of my disorder and just like in the doctor's office I sat there in my tea dress with a nervous smile and detailed my thoughts of decapitated children and torn vaginas. Before I left the assessment, she patted me on the shoulder.

The following month my award notice came in the mail and I found out I had been placed in the disability support group. I cried on the carpet with the letter clutched to my chest. I was safe for now. I had enough money to live. The fortnightly payments went into my Post Office account. I thanked my stars I lived in Scotland. I might have been dead somewhere else. I now had enough money to get by and a yellow slip of paper with the words Obsessive Compulsive Disorder on it. But after my diagnosis there was something else I had to accept the truth of. The dull ache in my left side. The empty bottles that stacked up through the years. The acid that leaked into my life.

I was an alcoholic.

And if I continued to drink after my pancreatitis it was going to be a long painful death.

Or a quick one.

Poison Draw

I knew without a doubt that drinking was going to kill me.

In my dreams I stumbled into a clearing where a blackened tree stood. It was full of rotten fruit. Malformed bugs with strange, crooked legs burst from the flesh of the spoiled juices, their bulbous netted eyes staring at me. I approached the tree with caution and tore the haggard fruit before being swarmed by a cloud of fettered wings.

Since the hospital I had continued to steal half cups of wine here and there. After my pancreatitis attack I had been caught in a furious tandem of staying dry for perhaps a month and then swinging back and rationalising a drink or two. Even this was too much for my body. After just one drink I spewed bile and the familiar dull ache returned to my side.

I never wanted one drink. I wanted ten. I wanted twenty. The only metric that mattered was more. The sweet numbing blackout was everything I desired. To escape my own mind. To find the elusive quiet. As the saying goes, "One is too much and a thousand is never enough."

I was faced with what seemed like a bleak truth – if I drank as I had done in the past my pancreatitis would turn chronic or into cancer, or I'd have a fatal narcotising acute attack and my pancreas would digest itself.

And yet in some electrochemical lunacy my brain still whispered reassurances.

I realised I was going to die and I still couldn't give it up.

I realised I was an alcoholic.

In my naivety I had a stereotypical view of an alcoholic. The lawyer sneaking vodka tonics in the shower. I thought in extremes. I was twenty-one years old. I didn't think this could be me or my life. But the bottles stacked up through the years and the alarming fact remained that even though I knew it would kill me I still was engineering excuses and in denial about my alcohol usage. And that was the very definition of the problem.

To wrench myself away from the label 'alcoholic' I used 'problem drinker' as it seemed softer. Easier to handle. This worked until it didn't – when a man in recovery told me, "You know non-alcoholics don't sit around and debate whether they like the term 'problem drinker' or 'alcoholic' better?"

I attended an AA meeting that was held in the basement of an old church. The trains were running late so I slinked to the back of the room. There was a man at the front sharing his story. He had greying hair and an old football hoodie on. There was a coffee break and I was quickly surrounded by people offering their hands to me. Strangers with kind faces clasping my hand in theirs and telling me I'd be okay. They looked at me with knowing eyes and asked me how long I'd been out.

I didn't know what that meant.

The folks at AA offered me coffee and their understanding. They assured me they had all been where I was and it would get better. I was overwhelmed by their kindness and thanked them all in turn. At the end everyone held hands and recited the

Serenity Prayer and though I didn't know the words I felt the weight of them.

"Grant me the serenity to accept the things I cannot change, the courage to change the things I can and the wisdom to know the difference."

I left the meeting with a copy of the Big Book tucked under my arm and the phone numbers of people who urged me to call them if I was feeling vulnerable. A lady walked out with me and as she lit up a cigarette she told me that no one is ever truly lost.

I didn't go back to AA but their kindness opened a door. Online I found a sober community. Stories were posted every day. There were archived threads of every struggle in sobriety from Day One to Year Forty. It was a community that stretched beyond time and space. I loved it. The community posts helped protect me from the kinds of things that can be especially volatile in early sobriety. The long term sober cautioned against following the tide of society. Things as seemingly simple as attending a party might be littered with triggers and the community helped me navigate them. I logged into the forum every day and typed the words: I will not drink with you today.

A simple sentiment that saved more of us than I can count.

Sometimes in those early days in my flat in Carluke, newly in sobriety, I would wake up and not know where I was. The world shifted and for a moment I'd think it had all been taken away and I was back in that place. The past strained to keep its hold on me. In unnerving nightmares I was cast back into dimly lit bars and clubs. Memories of dark places and shifting bodies. I'd wake, drenched in sweat, and the light would bring my small flat back into focus. I'd run my hands over my body and realise I was okay.

There were other poisons to extract from my life.

I met with Dad in a cafe a town over. He talked about some television show that was popular when he was younger. He talked about inside jokes with his friends. He talked about being head boy in high school. He talked about how good his grades were. While he talked, he played with the condiments on the table or looked past me to the window and the people on the street.

He didn't ask me anything.

His edgy inattention made me want to kick my chair back or flip the table. I wanted to cause a scene. Maybe then he might react or at least look me in the eye.

In the midst of his monologue he loused in, "I just think it's a bit weird how you went about it. Sneaking away."

"What? I wasn't sneaking away."

"Then why didn't you tell me?"

"Because you might have said no. You might have said I was too sick to go."

"Well truth be told I would have. You weren't ready. But your mum and you went ahead and what's done is done."

"I thought you'd be relieved. To have your own space."

"That's not the point."

My cheeks burned.

"I find it weird you let Lydia and I go to the hospital alone," I said slowly.

He lined up the sugar packets methodically on the table and brushed off what I said. "I thought your sister would be better. I was just getting in the way."

I searched his face. There was no flushing of shame, no embarrassment or regret. His eyes, grey like mine, were dark. There was no empathy in them. How could I talk to someone whose version of reality would always paint them as the good guy?

I'd heard it so many times before.

"I'm a good guy," Dad would say shrugging almost like his body was betraying the lie.

I have since learned that truly good guys don't have to tell you they are good guys all the time.

Dad spoke with the same clipped emotionality as he popped the first sugar packet back into the bowl. "It was very strange. You should have told me, instead of you and your mum having this secret plan. I've still never even visited the flat to make sure it's all fine."

I sat back in my seat.

That's not what you care about, I thought. You don't care about making sure I'm safe. You're just upset you didn't know.

"I was in a bad way and you let me stay and I'm really grateful for that," I said.

"Hmm."

"But it was hard. There was food in but not all the time. You would be at work and then watch television all night. You'd go to your girlfriend's for a few days and on the day you were meant to be back you'd say you're staying just one more day, and then another and another. I'd be alone. For a long time. And I wouldn't know when it was going to end."

In quick succession he threw each sugar packet into the bowl.

"I was scared," I said. "I couldn't sleep properly and I'd wake up with all the fights and drinking outside. And then I'd hide during the day because people looking for money would bang the door. I'd wait for you to come back and when you did – you didn't talk to me."

"I didn't know how to deal with you. What would upset you." His replies came back so deftly as if he had planned each in turn. "Jillian, we're not going to agree. You've said what you've had to and I've said mine so let's draw a line under it."

And so he drew the line.

I didn't know what I had been hoping for. That afternoon in the cafe I think all I really wanted was some small

100

acknowledgement from him. For him to see I was hurting. For him to say something, but he couldn't even manage that. We stepped outside onto the street and he avoided eye contact before breaking into the most disingenuous smile and saying, "There's my bus, I better go. Thanks for a brilliant afternoon!"

He ran across the road in his apprehension to get away from me and almost got hit by a bus pulling out from the stop.

Dad was there when things were easy. When he was on his second pint and I listened to his stories and fed him compliments just to try and get his attention. But he never asked how I was doing. That afternoon I realised something.

I didn't have to prove to him that he hurt me. In fact, my resolution couldn't be dependent on any sort of acknowledgement from him – because that would never come.

After all this time I'd gotten it so wrong. Life isn't a kind of television special where the main character reunites with their dad and after a few heartfelt words they reconcile and the end credit music plays. People are not owed anything simply by merit of being a parent. Especially if they have hurt you.

As for dads, I had been blessed with my stepdad. Jim had been a constant in my life; a steady influence keeping Mama going in difficult times and holding space for me. It was like he had been carefully fastening the ties of our own little family life raft, ready to keep us afloat whenever disaster should strike. Some modern scholars believe the phrase 'blood is thicker than water' might have been interpreted in the wrong way. They think that the expression could instead mean that people who have made a blood covenant or shed blood in battle together have far stronger ties than those born of 'water of the womb'. Interpreted this way it reads, "The blood of the covenant is thicker than the water of the womb." The blood that ties us doesn't run through our veins.

I liked that.

The poison of narcissistic abuse from Dad would flow in my veins for years after. I would have to unlearn guilt and self-loathing. But for now I had pulled the thorn from my palm and could begin to heal.

Sobriety gifted me the space to heal.

I found myself in what is known as 'the pink cloud'. The pink cloud is the period of sobriety when your body and mind have had enough time to withdraw from the alcohol and truly heal. As the dopamine centres in my brain became used to a normal level of stimulus I began to feel better than I ever had before. The euphoria enkindled every fibre of my being. On waking I didn't retch from rising bile and each nerve of my body wasn't clipped. The wave of despair didn't crush me and my muscles didn't seize and my head didn't roll like a stone. Instead I woke with a blossoming in the centre of my chest.

My body and mind were still, calm, an alkaline shore.

The ordinary, everyday things took on a new brilliance. Ramen Dayo in the city with my sister and Craig. For Eurovision I travelled to the cottage and as the bus passed through valleys of green I was startled by their verdancy. Was green always this green?

The dogs greeted me at the cottage and I patted their soft heads and kissed Mama and Jim. I set to work making little flags for the different countries. Benji the dog got Sweden and we all groaned as he looked rather smugly on. The last warmth from the dying sun, the music from the show and the joyful laughter of my family, even now I can't fully explain how much it all meant to me. The normality was everything. The pink cloud imbued everything in its soft haze and I could finally breathe.

In addiction circles the pink cloud can be seen as a bad thing. The elation doesn't last, the honeymoon period soon ends and as you shift back into regular life without the crutch of addiction you can be vulnerable. But the pink cloud showed me how good my body and mind could feel without alcohol. It showed me what really mattered. With the brief respite I was able to attend medical appointments, set up things in my new home and spend time with my family.

That night I fell asleep with the dogs beside me snuffling in their sleep. As I looked out at the violet sky, I couldn't have known that in just three short months I would meet the man I would fall in love with.

Joseph

His name was Joseph.

In early sobriety I found myself a little lonely. My body was healing from years of past abuse. Slowly opening like Lamprocapnos – the bleeding hearts flower. Without the suffusion of alcohol and shady bars I decided to do what I'd done when I was a teenager and reach across the static of cyberspace. I set up an online dating profile. At first it seemed like just a lark. I didn't really expect to actually meet someone but I figured it'd be nice to speak to someone new. To be open and vulnerable in that way you can only do with a stranger across the void.

But then his profile popped up.

A man with dark eyes, a beard and moustache in the style of a silent film villain.

When I saw his expression in his profile photo my heart did a weird staccato thud in my chest. There was a sadness in him and also something I couldn't quite put my finger on. He seemed too familiar. I peered so hard at his photograph that the pixels began to blur on the screen. Why did I feel like I already knew him?

A moment later a small dialogue box popped open in the corner.

It was him.

We sent a few awkward messages to each other. Tried to make one another laugh. We were strangers reaching out across the static void. Desperate to make a connection.

And we found one.

For a fortnight we spoke every night. Sharing small shards of ourselves and giving the other the opportunity to rip us in two. I half expected him to recoil when I told him about the thoughts but he accepted the circadian violence I described. With him I suppose I didn't feel quite so mad.

Joseph wanted to meet.

Love does not wait for a convenient time. It does not wait until you are safe, sane or settled. My heart had been dormant for so long and yet here he was. I would have never forgiven myself if I hadn't give it a chance.

One balmy summer evening we decided to go for a walk in the small town we both lived in. Hastily I put on my red dress and managed to spill half my bottle of perfume over myself before fixing my blush. I had no idea what to expect but I was tired of illusory plans and putting life on hold. Half an hour later I was running down the hill with my dress billowing in the summer night air.

Joseph strolled from under the glade and winked at me as if to say, "Hello, stranger. Hello, my old friend."

Before I knew what I was doing I had crashed into his arms and he pulled me close. The skin of his neck was still slightly damp from the shower and he smelled like dark caramel. It was a sweet homecoming. We walked around the streets until well after the orange lamplights flickered on. I hungrily watched him.

Warm from the heat, he casually took off his faded denim jacket and I saw his arms, strong and tattooed with blue flowers. He grinned at me when I told him I was three months sober.

"I did wonder when your profile didn't list a drinking preference. I'm in recovery too. Have you been to a meeting here?" He frowned. "No, I'd have definitely seen you."

He told me about 13th Stepping which was when someone with more sober time would pursue a relationship with someone brand new in recovery.

"Can create a whole bunch of issues. The power imbalance, you know? Makes for quite a toxic situation. In fact there's a general no dating rule across the board. It's not official or anything but really frowned upon."

"I thought people in recovery might be good together? They'd understand?"

He paused. "It can work like that, I guess. I think I've just seen it go the other way too many times. Folks get together and then one falls off the wagon and drags the other with them."

"That makes sense."

"For folks in AA they suggest not getting into a relationship for at least a year. People struggling with addiction are notorious for trading one bad habit for another. Heroin for alcohol, alcohol for gambling, gambling for sex, sex for food, you know? I guess we're all too good at using things to try to fill the void inside us." Joseph looked uncomfortable. "I don't know what to do. Three months in incredible, it really is, but you're still brand new."

"Oh," I said. "I didn't realise."

We stopped walking and I leaned against a wall beside the trees. The brick made little grooves in my legs.

"I wish you had a little more time," he said and smiled.

"Me too."

But I couldn't stand the thought that this might end before we'd even had a chance. I tried to clear my throat but my voice still caught as I said, "Listen I understand you wanting to protect my sobriety, I get that, I really do. But at the end of the day you know – it's not totally your decision to make."

The shadow of the tree branch seemed to carve Joseph's face into two. The light shifted back and forth. I ached for him to say something, anything.

"Fuck it."

Joseph burst out laughing – a growl, a big earthy sound that I couldn't help joining in.

"Fuck it!" I agreed through tears of laughter.

There was a dark bloom of exhilaration in my chest as Joseph pulled me towards him. There was an urgency behind his kiss and my body responded in kind.

Hours later he walked me to my flat and said goodnight.

"It's mad. But it could work." Joseph's eyes darkened. "Because if I'm being honest, whatever the rules, I know damn well I'd have been straight over if I'd seen you at a meeting."

* * *

I couldn't get Joseph out of my mind.

He burned in my skin. When he laughed I reached out and put my finger on that one cruel pointed tooth in his mouth that made him look wolfish. I wanted to drag my finger across it and cut deep enough to bleed. He sliced clean through the bone. Left me nothing but marrow and nerve. A mollusk without its coruscated shell.

Our first time together my palms kept sweating on the walk home. It had been two years since I had been with someone and it had never happened without alcohol. I waited for the thoughts to sear into my mind and flesh and cut off this sweet new desire. I waited, but they never came.

That night there was only him.

In Joseph I found all the things that I thought had gone missing. Wooded glens and dark fruit. My own body reclaimed. A sugar hollow. His body was home. I traced the tattooed shipwreck on his chest instead of the haunted curve of my body. Compulsion gave way and I found blue in the reds. In the aquamarine tails of the mermaids on his chest that I kissed. He responded by grabbing my leg and drawing a wolf on my thigh in permanent marker. It didn't wash off for a week.

Joseph was playtime.

My disorder was characterised by my need for control. In the bedroom I relinquished it and found an inky bliss. The lines of my body blurred. The line between pain and pleasure obscured. My body become home to taboos only whispered before. Sweet pain and dark spaces. The bruises blossomed on my skin like a peach. Shadows of his fingertips and teeth on my thighs. I didn't need make-up this time. I didn't want to cover them up. They were the soft reminders of what we shared. Moments where we lost ourselves in each other.

The sad abuse that once held my body prisoner didn't fade gently. It was exorcised. It was during my relationship with Joseph that I began to understand the truth of what had happened during those years. It was as if I was trying to tune into a specific radio station through static waves and I could finally make out the words.

I found connection with my body again. It had been a distant shore, somewhere I had a faint memory of, but now I knew every line and could tell you its story. Sex could be funny and sweet. It could be dark and intense. It was undefinable. An unknowable secret we all shared. But I had never had the chance to feel these things before and because of that there had been

108

part of me that seethed with anger. An anger I could neither channel nor contain.

Though my senses were overwhelmed with fresh delights – my obsessive compulsive disorder still followed me into the bedroom. Sometimes as I climaxed the blood-stained thoughts would pierce my mind.

Red.

But I let go.

Pain.

Pleasure.

It didn't matter.

I was all things at once.

And Joseph helped me.

He was craving.

A thirst never fully quenched.

He was steadfast.

And he kept me safe.

After he would check I was okay and run me a warm bath. He'd wrap me in a fuzzy towel on the bed and kiss my forehead and I'd drift in and out of sleep running my hands down my body just like I'd done on the damp blue bath mat when I was a teenager.

Our relationship blossomed. We shared stories and found echoes of our own in them. I tracked every flaw, every scar, every unmined darkness in his character and in all of it found something beautiful. He'd come out of the shower damp with a chunk of amethyst around his neck and my heathen heart smiled. He was the first person in my life to reach for my Röhrig tarot cards and the first to ask me about the strange symbols on the altar and the Egyptian Goddess I wore around my neck.

From shadow to light his soul vibrated with my own, harmonious in accord. He made me feel strong. In the end there was nothing to fear and I understood this was how it was always meant to be. Our nights together were like a secret jewel I stole away in my pocket rubbing my fingers against its grain.

The seasons clicked on and each one brought something new – something good. Our first summer together I was calm instead of agitated by the heat and swell of a sad city. Instead we took the train to Glasgow together. Baleful pigeons picked at the stone skulls of dead men as we stretched out our legs in the dry gravel of George Square. In the Modern Art Gallery, Joseph and I considered a piece of a giant cartoon toucan with a speech bubble that said, "Give a damn!"

It quickly became our favourite saying.

Give a damn.

I fell in love with Joseph. He led me to the centre of the galaxy where the satellites circled and the weight of the stars was above us. At the very centre of it, like two black holes, we began our dance and created our own dusty little universe from the ashes.

That Christmas Eve he told me he loved me and I wasn't afraid to say it back.

In Spring on the little patch of grass beside the church Joseph threaded a wildflower behind my ear and asked me if I thought they would chase us out for being dirty pagans but the ladies and gentlemen merely smiled at us on their way into the service.

We slept together in his bed. I wasn't used to sleeping beside someone and often I'd lie awake looking at the ceiling. I was never much of a good sleeper but in the stillness I was at least content to listen to Joseph's steady breath. But I had forgotten myself in my happiness. I had forgotten that obsessive compulsive disorder never lets you sleep. Not really.

The dawn would always bleed in and soon in a perverse trick of fate an obsession that had burrowed into my mind for years was about to find its way into reality.

And it was going to happen to Joseph.

Blinded

Ommetaphobia is the fear of eyes.

I had been consumed with obsessions of eye trauma and bodily mutilation for years and so when Joseph called me and told me his retina had detached I thought I would go mad. But I didn't. The funny thing about obsessive compulsive disorder is that it has nothing to do with reality. It is an illogical, spiteful disorder. The fear is the only real thing.

And something I've learned is that humans can survive just about anything.

The call came one quiet afternoon. Joseph's voice was muffled on the phone. He sounded strange. "Can you meet me at the station? I'm due in ten minutes."

In a flurry, I found an old jumper and ran down the hill to the station. I had arrived early and so paced back and forth trying to keep from imagining the worst. The train screeched to a halt and through the window Joseph sat with his chin tucked into his body and his flat cap pulled low. As he stepped onto the platform, I pushed through the wave of oncoming people to get to him. We stayed in each other's arms until the platform emptied and it was just us. Joseph burrowed his head into my jumper. He told me the doctor said his retina had detached. He started to cry and I held him. I promised him he'd be okay.

We walked from the station to his house and as he sat in the kitchen with his mum, I went upstairs and quietly locked the bathroom door behind me.

When did it start?

The eyes.

Those empty hollows. The bloody tracts of veins magnified during an opticians visit. I always had one pupil bigger than the other. Mama took me to the doctor to check it wasn't anything to do with my heart but the optician flicked the lights on and off a couple of times and told us everything was alright. I just had to wear glasses to balance out my longsighted eye and my shortsighted one.

Perhaps from the outside it seems strange. Where did it start? Shouldn't there be some way to track the obsession? Perhaps it would be easier if it was as simple as that. To tell you that there was some seed planted in my mind at a young age. But there isn't anything. There isn't anything because obsessions aren't rooted in reality. They are irrational. Unfounded pieces of electrochemical data that spark in our neural pathways. It would be much easier to point from A to B and show you some childhood trauma for my obsessions with bodily harm but in truth it was a latent gene that might never have turned on.

The day Joseph got the news about his retina I surprised myself with how calm I was. Eerily so.

In the bathroom I typed into my phone *retinal detachment* and braced myself. I read through all the information – the causes, the risks and details of the laser surgery that was required to stitch the retina back on. When I had finished, I washed my hands and joined Joseph in his bed and held him.

There was no terror – I didn't lose my mind – and the reason for this is that OCD and real life are so wholly unconnected. What was happening to Joseph had nothing to do with my obsessions. I expected images of Joseph with ruptured eyes to sprout in my brain but they never did. I was not afraid. Instead I was singularly focused on making sure he was taken care of.

He was all that mattered.

On the car journey to the hospital Joseph gripped my hand so tightly that even after we arrived there were still tiny imprints of his fingers on my skin. I remember placing my own fingers over the marks. They were almost the same size. As he was wheeled away from me, I wished I could batter past the doors and go with him but instead I could only crane my neck and shout that I loved him until he was gone.

A few hours later Joseph was sitting in bed with an eyepatch taped over his left eye crowing about how he looked like Nick Fury. I laughed with delight and held him. The doctor explained there were no complications and Joseph's retina had been successfully stitched back on. We manoeuvred him gently into the car and he lay across the backseat with his head on a pillow in my lap. The car wound its way through the streets and I stroked his hair. With each stroke my limbs grew stronger. I knew I had found my place. A fierce protection welled in me. Until he decided he didn't want it any longer, I would be the one to take care of him.

The days continued with small improvements, and we were content, but that October Joseph visited the optician for a routine check-up and found out the surgery had led to a cataract forming in his eye. I studied Joseph's face but he was quiet. It wasn't until we were outside the optician's that he said anything.

"It was always a possible complication. If the cataract gets any bigger I'll have another surgery but I'm not going to live my life in fear."

I buried him in kisses and he emerged looking pink and happy.

"You know, I think back to that surgery and in a way I think it freed me," Joseph said. "I was so scared of living in case it got taken away from me. But I'm not scared anymore."

Winter arrived with a sweet chill.

The sun disappeared before 4pm like a too quickly ripened peach and Mama and Jim slipped me an envelope with enough money for a new winter coat and a pair of boots. My feet were warm and dry as I crunched through the snows of a new season. With 80s Christmas tunes playing, Mama and I set to transforming the cottage. I donned my Santa hat and carefully untangled the lights for the tree and faintly heard Mama say something about Maya Angelou and how you can tell a lot about someone in the way they untangle Christmas lights.

Maya Angelou was right and I was about to learn what complete fools Mama and I were.

An hour later I was still at the lights so Mama suggested we cut the dead set off. We both agreed on the correct wire to cut and she snipped and a rush of hot water coursed down my hands.

How strange, I thought.

Mama and I stared at each other. All the lights had gone out. Immediately we realised our mistake.

We had cut the wrong wire.

I bounded over to switch off the lights at the mains and Mama and I stared at each other with the same guileless expression. There was a crackling of burning and the fillings in my teeth ached.

"Did you just... electrocute me... Mama?"

She looked in horror at the scissors. "Yes, darling. I believe I did."

We erupted into laughter and she put some chocolates in my pocket and I got back to work on the Christmas tree. I dressed it in the brightest tinsel and baubles – all the while the faint smell of singed hair burned in the air.

Living came with pain.

Beginning this new life only compounded anxiety's effects and with each experience it was as if I was scratching into my flesh. This life was filled with new blood and all the things I was hiding from – love, loss, fear and pain. But it was worth it. If living came with this as a side effect then, okay, I'd find a way to manage it along with the rest.

The Christmas tree was golden with a thousand firebugs caught in its green fronds. That night I laughed with Mama and her brilliant eyes crinkled at the corners. We spoke of the strangeness of this world and beyond. The spirits and sprites embalmed me in that place. In the small hours I crept along the wooden corridor to see the moon hang full like a glorious pearl.

My family and I watched films together as the fire spat auburn and I slowly drifted to sleep. Every day it seemed as if I was healing a little more. The distorted world of the past seemed a little further away. The fear was still with me, and the intrusive thoughts still bled into most hours of the day, but now there were moments of happiness to be found in-between. Life was about more than just surviving.

I had found sweetness in the dark.

One day Joseph and I lay on his bed and traced patterns on the ceiling like constellations in the night sky.

"Do you think we've ever crossed paths before? Walked by each other on the street in Glasgow years ago?" I asked.

"Definitely. Two strangers in a sea of people."

"I've always felt like this isn't our first time together. I wonder how many other lives we've had together. Who we've been to each other."

"In one we were probably two drunks down at the docks in New Orleans," Joseph said and laughed.

"I can see us toasting each other with our caps on!"

"Where else have we been?"

"Another Scottish life I bet. Maybe you were my wife this time and I was a great strapping Jacobean warrior!" I said.

"Oh aye."

"But I fell in battle."

"Well then I'd have to throw myself off a cliff."

"What do you mean?"

"Well I couldn't live without my husband." Joseph shrugged.

"I'd want you to live though. What if you jumped but you survived and ended up getting picked up by some wicked person?"

"Alright you."

I peeked out from the pillow. "What do you think this life is?"

Joseph paused for a moment. "Maybe this time there's no big trauma or separation or battle."

He brushed my cheek and said,

"Maybe this life we're just here to look after each other."

Predators

Theme switching is a common symptom of obsessive compulsive disorder. Just when you think you've got a handle on one kind of obsession, the disorder can shift in horrifying ways. Perfectionism, contamination, harm, symmetry and moral scrupulosity. Sufferers of obsessive compulsive disorder can vacillate between these different subtypes and many more but what is always present is the false guilt. The strange warping of reality. Because you will come to believe things you never thought possible. That is what this disorder does to you.

Obsessive compulsive disorder says:

Here.

Try this one.

The malignant paranoia was one of the most difficult symptoms I had to reconcile. There were times when I was acutely aware of how illogical I was being but in the moment the fear was so very real. Obsessive compulsive disorder painted the world in its own vile colours. It blackened the sky and made it so I was afraid to walk on the ground. And perhaps worse of all it convinced me that this was the only reality that existed.

I did things that in an otherwise rational state I could have never imagined doing.

A new compulsion took hold and I began carrying a water bottle everywhere I went. On the surface this might seem like a healthy habit but I can assure you hydration was not my concern. In fact I never took a sip from the bottle. That would have been wasteful. The water bottle served an entirely different purpose. One afternoon I was running some errands, wondering whether I should visit the post office or the bank first, and it happened.

Red.

A white heat burned across my face. My fingers touched my cheek and thick clumps of skin pulled away like white webbed moths. The toxic stench of the fire inflamed my nostrils. *I'm burning.* The fumes curled up in my throat and I heard strange screams reverberate in my skull until I realised they were my own.

Reality filtered in. The street was quiet. Just a couple of mums with prams chatting to each other and looking at me from corner of their eye. My dress was doused in sweat and I couldn't catch my breath. The next day I started to carry the water bottle. Every morning I filled it up at the sink with a blank, passive stare. Logically I knew how absurd my behaviour was but every fibre of my being told me it was the only way to stay safe. I was chained to my compulsions.

And as new compulsions took hold so did new obsessions.
Red.
People are dangerous.
You can't trust anyone.
They could be a predator.
They could be a paedophile.
The fear cleaved at my chest like a hacksaw.
Even your family could be dangerous.
You have no idea what people are capable of.

You can't trust anyone.

Keep to yourself.

You'll be safe then.

My mind fractured as the two realities fought each other. This isn't real, I thought.

It's the only thing that's real.

Sinking into that dark paranoia, I ebbed in and out of consciousness the whole day.

The next morning on the way to the shop I was careful to keep far away from the other people.

Red.

Monsters.

The paranoia subsumed me and I stopped going out to the shop for the next few days. I hid in my flat. It was difficult to return messages to my family. How could I possibly explain? The obsession never let up. Hours spent near catatonic with the same ugly thought repeating:

They are dangerous.

I hoped the warm water of a shower might diffuse some of the tension in my body but the water wasn't calming and in the naked space of the shower I become all too aware of my own body. I scratched an itch on my leg but the gnawing itch only grew. It hissed at me, insistent. It was as if there were thousands of insect eggs buried under my skin just waiting to hatch. I scratched my legs until red tracks grew deeper and deeper. The hot water seeped into the fresh grooves and stung. I tried to stop my hands but they continued to tear. When I finally pulled them away my nails were full of soft pink flesh. It made me think of a picture I once saw of a paper wasp nest – the holes agape like some pulled wound. I baulked.

The next morning something was different.

The onslaught of the predator obsessions usually began before I had even opened my eyes but this particular day was quiet. I anxiously surveyed the room not quite trusting it to be over. My phone was littered with notifications and I messaged my family and Joseph back. As the day continued I found I was able to breathe. With a little distance from the obsession, I was able to ground myself. I imagined great roots drawing forth from my arms and legs and pulling me down into the undergrowth. For a time I was able to acknowledge that my predator obsession was just that – an obsession. A lurid call of a voiceless fear.

Online I researched and found a certain theme or subtype of obsessive compulsive disorder known as Paedophile OCD wherein the sufferer believed themselves to be a paedophile. I read through their stories and felt such sadness for people who were close to taking their lives due to this obsession. There were also others like me who had become convinced that the people around them were paedophiles or predators.

It was as if obsessive compulsive disorder adhered to the old pillar of improvisational comedy: "Yes and...?" It took the most horrible things a person could imagine and told them they were true.

But there are more colours to the world than red.

The weekend after my first predator obsession Joseph and I travelled to the cottage to see my family. Mama told me I looked pale and I shrugged but I was struggling. This disorder could paint everyone I loved as a monster as if on a whim. It painted the whole world like that and wanted to keep me chained to it, dependent on it. It wanted me to rot alone in the flat, scared of fire and bone. It wanted to take everyone and everything from me.

It wanted me to die.

What a sick joke to have the people you love most, trust most, suddenly become devils in your mind, I thought. And if I tried to argue with the disorder it only grew. Obsessive compulsive disorder by nature is emboldened by attention.

121

Every little piece of reassurance and defiance I fed it, it happily accepted. Its every mechanism was geared towards continuing the desperate cycle of obsession and compulsion. The feedback loop only grew louder until it deafened me.

The only way I survived those days was by letting go. The only thing that stood a chance was acceptance. That weekend at the cottage with my family I sat in the corner and tried not to make direct eye contact with anyone for too long. I was scared my thoughts would make me lash out at them. My family were squashed together on the couches petting the dogs and enjoying cups of tea. I existed in a kind of twice blinded purgatory. I was both there and not. One half of me laughed and asked for another biscuit while the other disorder half remained vigilant and regarded them with hesitation. My OCD was uncertain they were who they told me they were. The paranoia was like a festering wound. It was then I accepted that it might be this way forever. That I might be this way forever. I would have to find a way to live with the obsessions like caged driftwood at the mercy of the tide.

But there is always a way to live.

One thing I knew I could trust in was this – there was hope – and when you can't hold onto it sometimes someone else can hold onto it for you. Mama motioned for me to come out of the corner and she bundled me up in a blanket. In my heart I knew who these people were. They were my family and whatever distorted lies OCD tried to tell me it could never take that part away. With Joseph and my family I was blessed to be able to see some kind of future however hazy it might have been. There was a future. One where I found some kind of solid earth. One where I lived – just like everyone else. Mama kissed me on the forehead and Joseph winked at me while feeding stray crumbs of lemon cake to the dogs and for a while it was quiet again.

* * *

That summer the OCD conference came to Glasgow.

I purchased a ticket and on the day became part of the pulsing crowd that snaked its way through the tunnel to the SECC. As I entered the centre I saw 'OCD' lit up in neon lights which made me giggle. It seemed so absurd that a venue usually reserved for concerts now had 'OCD(!)' as the headliner. At the stalls I held books and materials in my hands and wondered if somewhere in them there might be an answer. I had no idea where to go but soon spotted a fellow ginger, a man with a comic book t-shirt, and as he shuffled out of the hall I followed after him feeling like some shady stalker. I blurted out rather too loudly, "Is it alright if I sit beside you?"

He seemed amused but motioned to the seat next to him.

"Are you with friends or family or do you...?" he said, not quite meeting my gaze.

"Oh, yes, OCD! I mean – I'm the one with OCD."

"Me too."

"Brilliant!" I said before cringing at saying something so stupid.

The ginger man was kind though and just laughed. "Yeah, brilliant."

We were cut off by the first speaker who made a statement by licking his shoe – a stunt for sure but an admirable one from a man who had severe contamination OCD. Half of the room recoiled and half burst into laughter. Different psychologists took to the podium and I tried not to blink too much in case I missed something. At mid-morning break the ginger man, who I learned was called Tom, and I headed for tea and biscuits.

"The first round of CBT didn't really take. They can only offer you six sessions and then boom you're out the door. It's not their fault, just the way the system is. But then I found this

123

chap online in the States and I Skype with him now. He's amazing, honestly. Everything has completely changed for me," Tom said.

"I can't wait for my letter to come through," I said.

"What's that, two years? I bet it'll come soon and when it does it'll change things for you. I have ROCD – Relationship OCD – and I used to always second guess whether I was with the right person. I'd second guess whether they loved me or if I even loved them. It was a mess. Didn't matter what drugs they gave me. Therapy was the only thing that worked."

"I'm sorry. That sounds awful," I said.

"Yeah, wasn't great."

The other people in the hall were laughing or nodding their heads, deep in conversation with a stranger, a friend.

I decided to take a chance.

"My obsessions – they are quite violent."

Tom nodded insistently and I felt a wash of relief. "Oh man, I've had them," he said. "Sexual ones too. I always thought I was going to grab someone. I would never hurt someone so for my brain to keep showing me that – it was hell. But things are better now. We'll get through it you know. Another biscuit?"

I gratefully accepted the custard cream and as we walked back into the main room our steps were in sync with one another. I used to be so lonely. Years before it felt like I was seeing everything through a plane of glass, and yet, even when I tried to shatter it all the pieces of glass got stuck in my fingers and people still couldn't hear me. Now I understand how many of the same fears and anxieties we all share. In being vulnerable we give ourselves the opportunity to really connect with someone. A stranger – a friend. And it turned out Tom was right. Right after the conference as I walked along the tunnel there was a notification on my phone.

A psychiatrist called Dr Helen had called.

Sebastian and the White Bears

The day I met Dr Helen was the day I finally found some purchase in the resistant and difficult condition that is obsessive compulsive disorder. I had been working with mismatched pieces of information gleaned from the Internet and self-help books but it wasn't until I met her that I realised how in the dark I'd been. Thankfully she held the lantern for me. In Dr Helen's room there was a small cracked window, old pipes gulping in the background and a generic photo of a sunflower that beamed rather hollowly at me.

Dr Helen brought out a beige folder and studied it over her black rimmed glasses. I recognised it as my patient file. I had grown accustomed to reading through them at St Michaels. I shook my head like an etch-a-sketch and tried not to think of Dundee. Dr Helen noticed but merely nodded.

"I want to start by talking a little bit about obsessive compulsive disorder. There's a particular quote I think you might find interesting. Dostoevsky once said, 'Try to pose for yourself this task: not to think of a polar bear, and you will see that the cursed thing will come to mind every minute.'"

I smiled, "I wish they were only polar bears."

"Of course." Dr Helen smiled. "This quote was taken further by a psychologist who created an experiment where people were asked to talk for five minutes stream of consciousness style. The one rule was they were asked not to think of a white bear. Each time they thought of a white bear they were to ring a bell. The scientist found that though they were told not to the participants thought of a white bear more than once per minute. So this psychologist developed a theory called Ironic Processes to suggest that when the mind is trying to avoid a certain thought, one part of the mind does indeed ignore it but another part checks in to make sure the thought is not being brought to mind and in doing so –"

"Brings it to mind," I said.

Dr Helen clicked her fingers. "Exactly! Now mindfulness, exposure and acceptance have been shown to be the most useful tools in helping cope with these white bears or intrusive thoughts. There's been a lot of success treating OCD with a form of therapy called Exposure and Response Prevention where a patient is exposed to their fear gradually and repeatedly in a controlled environment and prevented from performing their compulsions until their anxiety peaks and tapers off. When this happens, the patient learns that they can survive. This is repeated until the patient becomes habituated.

Our work will contain some elements of exposure and a rejection of compulsions but I want to work with you using a different framework. I want to do something called Acceptance and Commitment Therapy with you. It will make a lot more sense as we go along so don't worry if this all seems a bit confusing just now. ACT focuses on decreasing avoidance and increasing psychological flexibility."

"Avoidance?"

"Yes. Avoidance is an unwillingness to experience particular thoughts, or go to particular places, and the need to escape painful intrusive thoughts or experiences. The avoidance is what maintains OCD. There is a cyclical nature to obsessive compulsive disorder. Compulsions feed obsessions, not the other way around."

She sketched out a circle with **Obsessions** and **Compulsions** linked by arrows.

"For example, the more you avoid knives for fear of bodily harm or violence the more you feed into the obsession. You tell your brain that it's right and so it repeats the loop. Coping behaviours only serve to reinforce obsessions. Does that make sense?"

"The more I avoid going outside, the more I tell my brain it isn't safe out there?"

"Exactly and then you become paralysed because there is an endless loop of obsessions feeding the compulsions and so forth."

"So what do I do?"

"You break the cycle." Dr Helen drew a line down the middle. "Everyone has intrusive thoughts. Mrs White from down the street waits at the train station and suddenly it pops into her mind that she could push the little girl in front of her onto the tracks. The difference is she doesn't interpret the existence of the thought as a moral failing. You know what she does? She goes, 'Oh that was a weird thought! Now what biscuits will I have with my tea when I get home?'

Intrusive thoughts are normal. Everyone has them. But the difference is when you have obsessive compulsive disorder the extent to which you experience these thoughts and the coping mechanisms you develop as a result become debilitating to the point of serious illness. A thought is just a thought, it doesn't have any intrinsic morality but how we interpret them is the real problem."

"So what do I do when those thoughts come in?"

Dr Helen sat back in her chair, "Don't fight it. Don't offer it anything negative or positive. Don't give it any energy, that only reinforces it. Instead acknowledge and accept the thought's existence. Oh I'm not saying it will be easy. In fact it will be very, very painful but you must do it anyway. Sit with it. Don't push it away."

Dr Helen fixed her eyes on me. "There is a key tenet to ACT, something the whole thing is based on and without it, it all falls apart."

"What is it?"

"That we aren't doing therapy to get better. Not in the way you think. That may sound strange but it's true. You must let go of the idea of control. You can't go into this with the same mentality you've had before because that hasn't worked. You cannot control this process. This might work and it might not, but we can't go into it seeking an end result. You need to truly accept that no matter how much we work at this you might never get better."

Therapy – without the hope of recovery?

Dr Helen caught me. "Now often times as a result of our work in therapy we have the happy side effect of improvement across the board but there can't be these tightly controlled goals here, okay? Trust me."

I had no other option and so I did.

At our next session Dr Helen peered over her black rimmed glasses at me.

"We're going to try something different today. I want you to practice gaining some objectivity when it comes to these thoughts. I want you to be able to create a little space, a little distance between you and the obsessions and hopefully once you have that distance you will be able to view them as what they are, thoughts. Just thoughts, not predictions or certainties. We need to remove their power over you and make them as mundane as the thought of starting dinner, alright?"

"That would be nice."

"Great! So, one of the ways we can do this is by identifying the obsessive voice and giving it a name."

"A name?"

"Yes, a name, in fact a whole personality! For instance, I call my obsessive voice Bob! Like in Blackadder, the way Rowan Atkinson says, 'Bob!' So then when Bob perks up I just roll my eyes and say, 'Oh here we go again, same old Bob with the same old story.'"

The idea thrilled me and yet I was fearful of it. How could I possibly reduce the blood-soaked images and thoughts to a name?

"It will be hard at first but I promise the more you practice the easier it'll become. In the beginning you might become very overwhelmed and your brain might try and protect you by rejecting the idea but if you keep treating the obsessions with a gentle sort of 'Oh here we go again' mentality, you might see a change."

"And yours is called Bob?" I chewed my lip. "Well, this might sound stupid but I think I have a name."

"Aha! Wonderful. What came to mind?"

"Sebastian."

"Why Sebastian?"

"Sebastian has a way with words. Sebastian is cunning, charming – almost snakelike. He can capture anyone's attention. I know that when these thoughts come into my mind I am completely taken in. The obsessive voice is so clever. So convincing that I believe it every time without question. Yeah, if my OCD voice had a name, I'm sure he'd be called Sebastian."

Dr Helen scribbled on my case notes. "It's perfect."

And so I began to call him by his name.

Sebastian.

It proved difficult at first. I tried to feign a nonchalance I did not possess as the intrusive thoughts tore through my mind and called out meekly, "This again, Sebastian? Really?"

In the beginning Sebastian did not react kindly to this. My stepdad said, "Well he wouldn't, would he? This Sebastian, all he wants is your attention and energy. It's how he sustains himself. Without that, what then? Of course he's going to fight back. But you need to hold on. You're doing so well, love."

Whenever Sebastian Red reared his head I sighed or pretended to shrug. "What now?"

Unfortunately obsessive compulsive disorder is an insidious affliction.

Let me show you.

Sebastian amplified and distorted the intrusive thoughts until I became blind to anything but them. He would play them in quick succession – bodies burning, headless children with their hands tied up with rope, the flayed skin of man sloughed from his body. That's how it went in those first days. For a month or two Sebastian used every trick up his sleeve. Every day was crueller than the last. Sometimes when he turned up I would mutter, *"Sebastian Red wants you dead."*

One day after the usual assault I could almost hear his exasperation. It wasn't working like it used to. That afternoon I heard nothing from Sebastian. That whole glorious afternoon I pottered around my flat able to read my book and talk with Joseph on the phone. I was free from any roaming demons. Just beyond the bitter side of hell was heaven and it was quiet there.

"I'm very pleased with the work you've been doing over the past few months."

I smiled. "I wouldn't have been able to do any of it without you."

Dr Helen clucked, "You're very kind and though I do appreciate it, at the end of the day when Sebastian turns up it's you who is dealing with him. The mindfulness techniques and naming exercise seems to be working well for you. Now I want to focus on what I think is a major piece of the puzzle. Have you heard of reassurance seeking?"

"Oh yes, I read about it in the therapy book."

"Ah well, any of it sound familiar?"

I nodded. "I know that sometimes when I'm triggered by something or have an intrusive thought I go to Mama. If I'm at home I send her a message or if I'm at the cottage I run through and ask her, "Will I be okay? And if I'm not okay will you still love me?"

"Seeking reassurance."

"She'll hug me and say all the words I need to hear – that I'm safe and that I can get through anything and that it's all going to be okay."

Dr Helen scribbled on her pad. "It's very difficult because on the surface this looks to be a completely normal behaviour. What parent wouldn't comfort their child when they are in pain? Indeed what human wouldn't offer another support if they saw them in such distress? But in your case, it is about context, Jillian. If you are going to your mother for comfort about what Sebastian is telling you, then we need to find a way to reduce and stop this behaviour."

"I know." I looked at the ground.

"Your mother can still be there for you. But the reassurance seeking is a coping mechanism like any other – a compulsion – and what do compulsions feed?"

"Obsessions." I met her steady gaze. "I know you're right. The reassurance never lasts long anyway."

"It's like a drug. You'll never get a hit like that first one and after a time you'll need to use more for it to even be effective. I know this is going to be tricky but I think if your mother and you can come together on this it could be very helpful."

At the cottage I explained to my family just like Dr Helen told me. They understood and promised to do whatever they could to help. That night before bed Sebastian visited, and on impulse, I ran through to Mama's reading room.

"What's wrong, darling?" she said and stretched out her arms for me.

I paused. "I don't think I'm allowed to ask for this."

Her hands twitched as she put them flat on her desk and grimaced. Anchored in the centre of the room, I swayed back and forth as the images punctured my skull. Tears spilled from my closed eyes.

"Oh, darling… are you sure?"

"I'm sure." I opened my eyes and nodded at her.

"It's hard, darling but we can do this. If it means you getting well, I'll do anything."

For the next few months we employed this new technique and tried to rewrite twenty odd years of instinct. Our pairing was strong and on the days Mama struggled with not being allowed to hug me, I remained steadfast. When I faltered she was there for me and refused to play Sebastian's games. Without words or physical touch, she helped me back to this world. I soon stole more and more time from Sebastian. Through therapy there were moments where I was able to cut the thoughts off at the

132

source, their dead shapes left to float aimlessly in my mind until they disappeared. Like a virus the cellular damage was too much and they ceased to be able to replicate. After what Dr Helen told me I had braced myself; it made sense to dampen my expectations for therapy, but perhaps in that acceptance the change was able to come.

Of course, Sebastian was still with me.

He was there when I travelled to the cottage. He was there on the rickety bus that crawled through the fields back to Carluke. He was there when I hugged my family and had dinner with Joseph. He played an old and familiar tune.

You're going to lose them.

Mama eyed me with her hands twitching against years of muscle memory.

You are going to lose everyone you love.

"I can't," I whispered.

Mama looked out the window with sad eyes.

"I hope this doesn't go against what Dr Helen says. I don't think it does because I don't think this is Sebastian. I think it's something else wearing Sebastian's clothes because I know what you are feeling right now. I don't know a single person who doesn't, my darling. It's the most human thing possible. You never think you're going to cope. But then you do."

"How?"

"The day I got the phone call that my dad had died I felt like the world had dropped out from underneath me. That grief – I didn't know how to process it or how to even function but you know what happened? Something so small. I heard you crying and the world pulled into focus. You were crying because you were hungry. You needed feeding. I had to keep going for you. We all find a way to keep going."

I hugged her. Her smile was bittersweet and she chuckled, "Now don't tell Dr Helen in case I get into trouble."

The phantom using Sebastian's voice receded and as he pulled back I saw his shape was much larger than I had thought. Sebastian was like a small annoying puppet in comparison to the blackness that swelled in the theatre behind him. Every human knows that darkness intimately. I nodded at the shape, knowing before long it would come for more of my family. But for now, as Mama said, we all find a way to keep going. Though there was pain, there was also joy to be found. Cuddles with Joseph and nights at the cinema. Living room picnics with the family and furry-legged friends whose soft noses snuffled in the night. New books and fresh laundry and tea late at night when the world was still and everyone you loved was sound asleep.

Obsessive compulsive disorder is a chronic condition. Sebastian and I would be tied together forever. But therapy and Dr Helen taught me that the thoughts cannot hurt me. Somewhere deep down I always knew this. Whenever I would read or watch stories of people who had experienced trauma, people who might have lost limbs or been born without eyes or burned, no obsessions ever leaked into my mind.

It was just like with Joseph when his retina detached. My heart was steady and without fear.

During therapy I found a YouTube channel called Special Books for Special Kids that was filled with stories of people who lived life in another kind of way due to their disabilities.

Truthfully, I braced myself for the intrusive thoughts to flood in. But they never did. Instead as I listened to their interviews I found connection in their stories. A seven-year-old boy with no eyes snuggled into his mama and talked about how much he loved kittens (very fluffy kittens in particular). I couldn't help but smile. There was no fear. No phobia or obsession.

That is when I truly understood it was never the actual content of my thoughts that was harmful. In my heart I knew that people were resilient and could live through pretty much anything – it was the thoughts themselves that were the only threat to me.

Physical trauma was such a small part of these people's stories. When watching the story of a boy who had been burned when he was younger, it would have been perhaps easy to reduce his life to a single violent event without considering the same banalities of life that affected him. Like any other teenager he spoke about getting frustrated with his parents and in his free time making music on his laptop.

Funnily enough the next Special Book episode was about someone with OCD.

I was never alone after all.

The beauty of a quiet, normal life is not one only afforded to those without trauma. And I wonder if anyone is truly without trauma whether it lines their physical, emotional or spiritual bodies. I believe, like the Japanese art of Kintsugi which repairs broken pottery by filling the cracks with gold, there is beauty in such things. In surviving and lacing our wounds together with golden thread we become even more than we might have been.

Poppy and the Bean

In all the obsessions, somehow you never imagine the real tragedy. The sleeping misery that creeps up and chokes you. It began with a flourish, a pink bloom, the faint double line that told us that bedded in my sister's womb there was life.

Lydia lined up all the tests in neat little piles and asked us to double, triple check – to hold them to the light to see – but we didn't need to. It was clear. Life took on new shape and meaning. We started to make plans and buy small outfits. Lydia brimmed with joy as she told us that the baby was now the size of a poppy seed.

But then the world turned.

Lydia started to have pain and abnormal bleeding. Craig messaged us to come over and when he opened the door he was small and grey and Lydia was bundled up in blankets. Her eyes had changed. There was an impenetrable sadness and something inside her had shifted forever. She and Craig would never be the same. We stayed on the couch together as the last of the winter rays left us.

That week I stayed with Lydia and Craig. He worked quietly in his room and I brought him cups of tea and soup and he nodded his head. I wished there was more I could do for him, something I could say. Lydia rested in bed and I crawled under the duvet beside her. We talked when she was able to and just lay together when she grew quiet. Her hands traced over her stomach. When Lydia fell asleep, I squeezed my eyes and imagined Poppy on her new journey, a bright universe lying before her. I remembered the fabled world of the children of mortals and gods who rested in a state of pure bliss and whispered, "Go join the elysian."

The late winter snows flurried as Lydia took her first walk. She trudged up the hill with her mouth set firm and her face red. After that it became too dangerous to go outside so we cuddled up in bed together and let time slip past us. Lydia cried. What started as a crack down her face became an aching howl as she pressed her face deep into the pillow. All I could do was hold her. Mama somehow cleared the snow. She had a care package prepared and one of the items was a silver ring box. Lydia nodded and Mama put Poppy's remains in the little box and we buried her under the rockery garden. Lydia marked Poppy's place with a plastic tulip, two-toned pink and red with its flower quite upright.

The months passed and Lydia and Craig slowly stitched themselves back together though the thread was so delicate that a small tug threatened to loosen it. We had family lunches and talked about Poppy, remembering that Craig and Lydia were still parents.

Soon there came hope, the fresh bloom of a double pink line – a new blossom in her womb. We were cautious but soon allowed our joy to spill over and started readying ourselves with plans and small outfits, mostly in blue or green as Lydia was convinced the baby was a boy. A brother for Poppy who we called Bean.

In all of our excitement we were pulled back to earth and the tragedy choked us once more. Craig and Lydia's tiny Bean left us. Their second child in spirit now with his sister. Lydia climbed back into bed. I didn't know how they would bear it but somehow they managed. The days clicked on and they found a way to climb out of bed every morning. Small laughs sometimes escaped before the sadness caught them again. They moved forward into an uncertain future.

One day in May Lydia was out in the garden hanging the washing when she was surprised to see one solitary tulip growing beside the plastic one. She was breathless on the phone to me. "You don't understand – there's never been a tulip in that spot before! We haven't planted any bulbs and yet the size and shape is just like that of Poppy's tulip. It's even the same colour, the same hues of pink and red."

Mama stirred from her nap to hear the tulip story and told us in her dream she felt someone come for Bean, to claim him and to name him. David. From then on we affectionately called him David Bean. We put a rainbow windmill in the rockery for him beside the tulip. Even without a hint of wind the windmill stirred wildly, and the tulip stood proudly beside her twin. The garden held space and time for our Poppy and David Bean. They would always be with us.

A particular bee often visited the tulip, climbing inside and falling asleep with its bum covered in golden pollen. He became a regular visitor. He was there when Lydia took a pregnancy test and we discovered she was pregnant again. A few weeks into her pregnancy Lydia and I visited mama at the cottage. Lydia had silver marks beside her eyes and though she was tired and nervous she seemed happy.

"It's like I've a bee in my tummy!" she said and laughed. "They seem so excited."

Lydia and I visited the hospital. I had watched the scene so many times before in films and television shows. The squirt of the jelly on the belly, preceded by the warning, "This will be a bit cold!" The nervous look in the mother's face and the euphoria when the picture lit up on the screen, the black folding back to reveal a little white bean, shuffling back and forth. I couldn't stop laughing as this weird alien creature bobbed their hands about as if to say, "I'm here, hello! It's me!"

It was a new beginning.

Every day Baby Bee grew stronger. Lydia proudly dressed her bump in blush coloured lace dresses. Fear still lined her face and in the odd look you could catch a gnawing panic but she was quick to distract us with another fact about Baby Bee.

"You know they're the size of an avocado now?"

"Little avocado. I must admit I thought it was funny when they looked like a small dinosaur. When they're older I can't wait to tell them about when they were a little shrimp."

Lydia pinkened with pleasure. "Do you think they like me?"

"I think they love you."

She turned to the window with her hand on her bump, and I could neither read nor understand the emotions that swam through the tides of her eyes.

* * *

At this time in my life it was the smaller moments that took hold in my heart; a quiet sun burning brighter with each passing day. The fear never completely left me, but it was different now. Life was still impossibly fragile but there was something miraculous in it. The past portrait of the girl was gone and I began moving beyond the confines of the frame, life no longer reduced to a static image.

There were reasons to live.

Lydia was taken to the hospital and Mama and I visited her before her inducement. The ward was quiet and Baby Bee was coming to meet us all. A group of cheerful midwives took over and ensured us that Lydia was in the best hands.

It began as soon as the car door shut behind me.

Sebastian hitched a lift in the back seat and whispered in my ear the whole journey. He showed me my sister bleeding out and Baby Bee being delivered without a head. But Mama needed me to be steady; I had never seen her look so ill. This night was about tending to her fears and soothing her while her daughter was in the hospital. After she was settled in bed, I closed the door behind me and Sebastian sat by my side all night long.

The next day I saw the first photograph. Lydia dressed in a gown flecked with spots of blood, smiling weakly, and there held close to her chest was Baby Bee in a small blue cap. The world righted itself and Sebastian shrugged and told me it wasn't over yet but I dismissed him with a quick wave of my hand.

At the hospital Craig beamed with pride as he introduced us to his son. Lydia was high on the drugs they had given her and although floating on another plane of existence, she was content. "You're here. Come say hello."

She shifted her shoulder and unveiled the missing piece of us. Baby Bee, now known as Alexander. Lydia adjusted Alexander's small blue cap and looked at him with fierce protection. I moved closer to the bed and rested a hand on his tiny body.

"Hello, Alexander, it's your Aunt Pea."

In that moment I felt myself shift out of focus. In the sprawling family tree and the edges of time the infinite became finite, and I found my place. It was here and now. I was part of the canvas of time that stretched on long before me, and far after.

Craig had always been gentle and kind, and those qualities translated to something quite remarkable in a father. In the pitched rays of the last sunlight, I watched him, Lydia and Alexander snuggled up together, a golden aura surrounding them. It was unquestionable – we are yours and you are ours. What they had now was something beautifully cryptic to me and I marvelled at the creation of their own little universe.

Alexander grew stronger every day. For a time he looked like a kind of garden snail, sweetly cooried into my sister. She played with him and pecked at his cheeks with her chest full like a proud mother puffin.

I had never seen anything so strangely familiar as if this is how it always was. Always had been. She was built for this, my sister.

"Do you think he's okay, Pea? Is this normal? I want to keep him safe forever."

"You're doing beautifully," I said.

Lydia left the room to quickly use the bathroom and Alexander wriggled on his baby mat with his eyes fixed on me. For a moment I hesitated.

Perhaps I should wait until Lydia returns? I thought.

Alexander was so tiny and I was terrified I would hurt his head or neck. But he made my decision for me. He furrowed his brow at me and in a moment he was in my arms where he cosied into me as if to say, "See, that wasn't so hard after all."

I held him close and smelled his sweet head. That Spring brought my family happiness like nothing else we'd ever felt. It had been a year of grieving Poppy and Bean and of worrying about the small Bee in my sister's womb. To finally have him here meant we could all catch our breath.

I held Alexander close and felt I had stolen some time away from Sebastian. He was nowhere to be found on that sunny afternoon. But I shouldn't have been so naive. In truth my obsessive compulsive disorder would always be with me, and only two days later it was going to shift again in another unfathomable way.

Tics

Tics with a c, not k. I wasn't possessed by tiny bugs but instead gripped by unexplainable jerks and spasms. They began as motor tics. My arm would be wrenched by a convulsion. I'd hold my arm close to my chest only for it to break free and hit underneath my chin. A particularly painful one was my neck snap. It would snap back repeatedly, often leading to terrible headaches the next day like I'd been hit by a truck. I had been consciously hitting my head since I was a child but now it was as if I were possessed by a demonic entity. It frightened me to be so out of control. I had been told the same things for years, that OCD couldn't hurt me or the people I loved, that it was a neural, chemical thing that only existed in my brain.

But it was leaking out of my body like radiation.

I was like a mechanical octopus, arms sparking and head fried. It became difficult to move without punching walls, or myself or throwing my phone off the wall. Joseph was concerned. "Is there nothing we can do?"

My doctor was brilliant. She prescribed medication to slow the tics and referred me to Neurology. I was terrified I might hurt someone, but she sounded dead certain when she told me that wasn't going to happen.

The next day in the kitchen, I tic-ed with a knife in my hand.

It was as if someone had burned my skin. I dropped the knife and backed into the corner of the room like a nervous dog. I was grateful that Joseph was nowhere near me when I tic-ed but my anxiety skyrocketed as I imagined that I could truly hurt someone by accident. Fresh terror coursed through my body.

It took the new medication and pulling everything I had learned from my therapy sessions with Dr Helen to make it through. I came to understand that the tics were new manifestations of my obsessive compulsive disorder. I couldn't find much information online but there were some people who experienced tic-related OCD. It was like when I'd shake my head like an etch-a-sketch when an intrusive thought came into my mind except on a more heightened level. I reasoned that if I treated the tics like I did with my obsessions and compulsions that it might work. The waiting list for Neurology was long and so I didn't have much choice but to figure things out for myself in the meantime. And so I practised Acceptance and Commitment Therapy techniques. I played dead. I created space. I was mindful.

I let go.

And a week later the tics subsided.

For a while at least. The pattern of tics were like fractals. I had more intense hours within more intense days within more intense weeks within more intense months. It reminded me of a Spirograph. There were pockets of time where the tics were acute but then others when I had some respite from them.

From some darkly absurd place I almost wanted to laugh. As soon as I had gotten a handle on a particular obsession, I experienced theme shifting. Then as soon as I finished therapy

144

and the frequency of obsessions diminished, I began to experience tics. Whole elements of the disorder changed right in front of me. It was like an alien language that kept changing. I only had a few books and my doctor to help me understand it as the disorder shrank and then blossomed into something new and altogether stranger.

But I suppose that is life, and though the tics were difficult to bear at times, at this time in my life I was happy. Being an aunt to Alexander made me see the world as he might.

Full of new colours.

In Joseph I had found a partner to face the wilderness against. One night we headed into Glasgow and returned home on the morning train engaged.

And there were other happy surprises. For one – my cognition was returning. I was able to read again. This also made it possible to attend occupational therapy. My therapist explained that it was about adding a little each day while still allowing for the days where I was impaired by my disability.

I signed up for short course focused on mental health activism in the community. It was my first time doing something that felt vaguely solid in a very long time. The class had eighteen different people and I felt held by every single one of them. Everyone was fiery and passionate and I was humbled by them. Some were mothers and fathers who had their own families and jobs and yet still worked tirelessly to make things better for those around them. Some were on disability like me except they picketed every weekend and demanded equality for their communities. The last group, me and a few others, were simply people with a lived experience of mental illness who wanted to help even though we weren't quite as well versed in policy changes. We were all of different races, religions and backgrounds and in that room we came together as one. They were patient with me and helped me find my voice again when I thought I had lost it.

There was a small certificate presentation ceremony at the end of the course and Joseph demanded to be in the front row. Curiously, on the evening of the presentation I found myself in a familiar place. At the top of a grand staircase, my fingers lingered on the polished wood. The spires stretched on to the very heavens themselves, the ribbed vaults reminiscent of a chapel. Outside the window the same fairy tale stone. The place I had tried so badly to find happiness. The ceremony was held at Glasgow University. I couldn't help but be amused at the funny loop my life had made. The same chord progression leading back to the very beginning. If only I were to hear my song now. Part of me expected the university to feel hued out and grey but there was too much emotion in that place. The same ghosts that haunted Dundee lurked here – ethereal past selves floating down the corridors with dark and hungry eyes.

"You doing alright?" Joseph asked as he slipped his arms around me.

"I'm doing much better," I said.

He held me and I felt the warmth of his body and good heart. One by one I met the gaze of each of the ghosts and in doing so freed them and they cast off into shards of light, spinning up to the spires above. I closed the chapters of Glasgow and Dundee and even Hamilton.

I was pleased to see that they only really took up the first few pages anyway.

A place opened up on a farm at Lanark with an organisation that helped people with disabilities. On my first day I opened the shed and was confronted by mouths of metal. Hacksaws, bow saws, Spear and Jackson loppers. Sebastian gloated as I tried to hide my tics and got to work filling a wheelbarrow with the tools we needed.

I worried that my boots looked too new and scuffed them on the ground when no one was looking. We took the minibus to Maudslie woods and the path to the clearing was filled with roots. I tried to be careful but when I tripped, three different pairs of hands reached out to catch me. A volunteer handed me a cup of tea and it was one of the best I'd ever had. Another made wolf noises and we all joined in. We huddled round the fire with our faces flushed and munched companionably on soggy biscuits.

I was surrounded by people who also had mental health or learning difficulties. There were no harsh lines of division drawn. Everyone was a volunteer and some of us just needed a little more help than others. We gathered firewood and spoke about wolves and shapeshifters and the mysterious procession of brown spiders by the oldest tree in the forest. When the team leader asked me how I had gotten on at the end of the day, there was dirt smeared all over my face and my hair was exploding out of its plaits. I'd been bitten by midges, taught how to fell a tree by cutting 'a bird's mouth' into the trunk and gotten to yell, "Timber" unironically.

"I loved it," I said, grinning.

A few weeks later I was paired up with another volunteer called David. He had learning difficulties and autism and wore noise cancelling headphones and thick gloves. On our first meeting I approached him gently and he too was cautious, peering out from under his hat. When he learned of our shared birthday, I saw the effortlessly mischievous grin that I would soon come to know as the David smile. One morning in the sensory garden he grabbed an axe and began chopping down a tree while laughing. I spoke to him softly, being careful to use his name to bring back his focus, and as I removed the axe from his hands he blinked at me like he had been some place far away.

"I'm sorry – didn't mean to..."

"It's okay, David. Everything is fine."

He looked up from under his hat. "Are you sure?"

"Definitely. You are safe, and look at that, we've brought the sun with us. We're going to have a lovely morning. Would you like some tea?"

He sighed in relief and after our tea we potted potatoes together while he held my hand and told me stories.

"You know I used to wish I'd never been born. I used to think it'd be better, that everyone would be better off without me," he said while digging with a trowel.

"That makes me sad. I couldn't imagine you not being here."

"I'm glad I stayed. I stayed for my mum but now I'm glad I stayed for me. Life is hard. Very hard. I wish I could do more – I can't read, can you read? I wish I could read and go places. You know I can't go on the train or travel alone? Mum says I wouldn't know when strangers were being bad or nice or me. It's hard to tell those things. They might take me away. I wouldn't want that. I want to stay with my mum. She reads me stories. The sun is very pretty today. You know with your hair in braids you look like a strong Viking lady. I saw a Time Team the other day with that man and they found Viking relics!"

"Maybe we'll stumble across an old relic while we're planting these potatoes! How good would that be?"

His eyes grew wide.

"David there is so much you can do. You're better at gardening than anyone here. Just look at the trench you've dug out. It takes time for everyone – you're no different in that regard. Just keep going. Know that every day you bring so much joy to people," I said as he peered at me from under his hat.

He gripped my hand tighter and popped a potato in the same hole I'd placed mine. I ended up tic-ing and David saw but he didn't care. It was okay.

He understood.

Home

A single light appears above my head. From its ephemeral centre, it slowly grows, the light splintering thread-like, until a single strand of pure white pulls forth. The thread weaves its way around my skull and loops close to my body. I am aware of a sudden pressure on my ribs, a heavy comforting weight. From my right side I feel the legs of a giant dusty brown spider working deftly, her eyes bright and keen. She finishes at my feet, pulling the loop of the thread closed and I am bound in a cocoon of light. I thank the spider and she moves off into the night.

I wake from the dream.

No longer are my nights filled with blood. Between the nightmares there are gifts of gentler dreams. A kind of harmony winds its way into the canvas of my life with new thread, or rather a thread I thought limited that proved to be without end. Mama is right; the heart is an infinite thing. And though it might hurt to let yourself be vulnerable, it is a wonderful kind of hurt.

My volunteer placement at the farm in Lanark comes to and end and I take the kindness I have learned from the volunteers with me. It is time to move on. I find a volunteer position one day a week doing archival work at New Lanark. It is a funny thing working on a historical site. People from all around the world travel to visit the heritage site and I have to admit I experience a swell of pride about Scotland. Before my shifts I wander through the buildings and their steady weight through the years assures me of something – that perhaps there are some things that can hold fast this chaotic world.

The oral histories I transcribe are recorded in the 1980s and most of the participants were in their seventies and eighties at the time. It's strange to think that they are probably not around anymore. The tapes sometimes stop abruptly halfway through one of their sentences and there is a stark silence. It is often jarring. It is a privilege to share in their story and to hear possibly their last words on tape. I can't stop the hippie part of me imagining where their souls are now. I do the maths and expect some of their spirits are back on earth again. I'm tickled by the idea that by some strange synchronicity they have landed back at New Lanark, a tourist child wholly unbothered by the secret history that lingers so close to them. Far more concerned about when it's time for ice cream.

I type all day on my rattling keyboard. Life in all its lightness and dark – the time their husband didn't come home from the war followed by a story about when cotton flew down the Clyde in great white puffs and every man, woman and child had to chase after it.

Sometimes their stories make me cry and I'm grateful to be alone in the archive room, but mostly they make me laugh. They remind me of the absurd nature of life – and what else is there to do but smile?

On the bus I listen to music and watch my rose gold ring catch the sun. When I come home to Joseph it just as wonderful as the first time.

I continue my frequent trips to the cottage but also free myself from a certain amount of separation anxiety. I realise my family are connected by a lyrical path of nature's sonnets, dark and deep roots, and that wherever we might find ourselves, we'll always be together.

One day as we are gardening Mama pats my hair. "Such a colour. Like copper wire."

She smiles at me as I use the clippers to deadhead the flowers in the garden. Except this time the metal doesn't sear my hand and mind.

"Funny how things change," she says.

"I was thinking that the other day. The year I was at my lowest – it was only seven months later that I met Joseph."

"Funny that."

"Seven months," I say. "That's all it took. You always say how quickly things can change and you're right."

"I never had any doubt you know."

"Hmm?" I look up from the flowers and smudge dirt across my nose.

"Mucky pup. I said I never had any doubt."

And she was right.

Things do get better.

Now I'm able to live beside Sebastian and the disorder that kept me from the world for so long. There are blues amongst the reds. There are cruelties in the world but there is also immeasurable kindness and I can only spend so long being unhappy. I refuse to self-cannibalise while there is a future out there waiting for me.

On Sundays I read the paper and particularly the uplifting news section – stories of everyday human kindness that tend to get lost in all the noise. Sebastian and I are still irrevocably tied. Obsessive compulsive disorder is an incurable thing but that doesn't mean it's not possible to live and live very well.

When Sebastian whispers in my ear I let go and turn my attention to the things that truly matter. Joseph. My family. These people are everything I am. How do you begin to try and thank someone for saving your life? How do you thank seven of them?

They stitched up my bloodied wounds and laced them with white light. They drove in the night to pick me up and take me somewhere safe. They understood when I needed help even when I couldn't speak the words. They comforted me after bad dreams. They found some kind of worth in me when I couldn't bear to be in my own skin. They were endlessly patient. They held onto hope for me when I couldn't and loved me without condition. They gave me a reason to stay.

Words return to me and for the first time in years something grows from the arid plane of the blank document. I'm still not quite sure why I'm writing this book. Maybe it's to make some sense of that time and to pull the faded curtain on this particular set of scenes. I know it's time to move on.

All that's left is the letting go.

A memory, almost lost, comes to me one day. One spring morning when I was seven or eight and eating sugary cereal on the kitchen counter, Mama yawned in her slippers and robe and popped on the kettle for coffee. With a mouth full of cereal, I chirped to her, "I couldn't sleep last night."

"Oh darling was it a bad dream?"

"Nope. Just couldn't sleep. Closed my eyes but then I kept thinking about dying and I got so excited."

In the middle of rubbing sleep from her eyes Mama burst out laughing. "What do you mean, darling?"

"I just got so excited. I couldn't wait to see what was next. It's like this big mystery that we don't know. Or maybe we do and we just forgot. But at some point you die and then you get the answer. In that in-betweeny place you get to find out what it was all about. Isn't that cool?"

Mama kissed me on forehead. "I understand, darling, but I hope that you get your answer when you're a little old lady tucked up in bed after a wonderful life."

After we are finished in the garden I kiss Mama, wave goodbye to Jim and take the dogs for a walk through the rust-coloured woodland. Rain falls in muslin curtains of water and tiny moths scatter like dust in the wind. There's a stump of a tree I sit on while trying to keep the dogs from licking various mushrooms. I think back to becoming nocturnal as a child due to sheer curiosity.

In truth I've never been afraid to die – what I really feared was living.

Maybe I'll be afforded the privilege of growing older, maybe not, but when the great curtain draws back and the lines between this world and the next blur the only sadness will be forgetting for a little while.

Faith is not a requisite to recovery. This disorder is a toxic thing of the mind but it is not without weakness, and with the right tools – therapy or medication – there is the hope of recovery for everyone.

There are all kinds of ways to live a life.

Perched on the tree stump with the dogs gambling around my feet I spy smoke blossoming from the chimney of the cottage and I know there is a fire to come home to. In the gloaming, Sebastian is still with me. He always will be. And that's okay. A pale moon crescents, waning on the right side, and bathes the horizon in a strange light. Something stings at my ankle and I realise the brambles in the undergrowth have left little scratches on my skin. I trace my finger over the marks. I am grateful for this body and its blood – its messy transience is a remarkable thing – a beautifully human thing.

For a time I find myself content to live in a bright kind of darkness.

How Blade in the Shadow came to be

I often wondered, while writing the last draft particularly, how someone else would come to view the book. I believed for years that I wrote for the pleasure of it. And indeed, it's true. Writing is like a strange alchemy and every morning I sat at my laptop with frizzy hair and wide eyes and tried to create something from everything that had come before.

As much as I love that kind of witchcraft – the delight of pure creation – it wasn't enough. I wasn't content to just print my story and leave it to ash in a drawer.

I craved a reader.

I wanted to be seen.

This perhaps shouldn't have surprised me. But it did. Stories need readers. There is something in the liminal space created between reader and writer. When the tiny letters shift and turn into shape and sound. When they become so much more than they were in the first place. That part is everything.

And so when Julianne read my book, I felt seen. When she found the title from a line in chapter two, she helped distil its very essence and everything else fell into place.

'Blade in the Shadow'

That existential fear. That creeping anxiety. That threat that never fully realises.

Filmmaker and painter Akira Kurosawa once said, "In a mad world, only the mad are sane."

In our modern world we are subject to a continuous level of anxiety like the white noise of a fridge running in the background. That constant hum of dread is the soundtrack to our daily lives. The mundane casually exists beside the cruel. We make a cup of tea while the world is on fire.

Inequality, poverty, climate change, government corruption are only a few of the ills of our world. The untamed garden seems too much of an undertaking for just one person. Though the content of my obsessions have little to do with reality, I can't pretend that the environment we live in hasn't presented the unique conditions for them to flourish. At my most unwell I saw only the violence in the world – and that is exactly what my OCD amplified until the world lost all colour but red.

The book may focus on OCD and addiction but in truth it's a story about healing. About embracing the elemental pain that comes along with living. Of knowing the darkness intimately and choosing to stay anyway.

'Blade in the Shadow' courts the fears we all are scared to name. Being a human being is a painful, bloody mess. A beautiful one for sure. But none of us make it through this without being wounded and in writing the book I was able to recontextualise the trauma I had been through. As cliché as it sounds this was a deeply healing process. I was able to make some sense of the years that had come before and now, in turn, I feel more confident that I can shape my own narrative going forward. The future seems boundless. There are so many pages left to write.

When I began to pitch my book I often felt I was playing some kind of pretend game. My mind told me I was worthless, that my story wasn't worth anything – who was I to be so arrogant to think I could write a book? But I've come to learn that telling your own story is a deeply powerful, even political, act. If you have been gifted a voice – it is your duty to use it.

While writing 'Blade' I was saddened when I stumbled across little puzzles and mini games with the hashtag 'OCD'. It made me sick that it was being used in this way. I thought of the disorder I knew – the one that haunted sufferers with obsessive thoughts that they'd killed their family, that they were a paedophile or of feeling so dirty they'd rip off their skin – and I couldn't reconcile it with the pastel-coloured photographs of neatly arranged sock drawers. Their ignorance revolted me and my sadness soon turned to anger. That is the place from which the first chapter of the book 'Knives' comes from. I wanted to show people what it was really like. I wanted them to spend a day with me as these obsessions destroyed my sanity. After that, I dared them to use the phrase "so OCD" again.

Telling my story was therapeutic and in some small sense, an act of rebellion, but it was also a plea for representation.

When I was younger one of my favourite episodes of the television show *Scrubs* was one where actor Michael J Fox played a character with OCD. Every time I saw it I quietly cried for five minutes. It's ending sees the character emotionally drained from his job at a new hospital and unable to escape the compulsive loop of washing his hands and flicking off the light switch. Actor Michael J Fox suffers from Parkinson's and imbued his performance of this character with his own pain – the sum of which creates an incredible emotional climax. And yet, I still didn't recognise that I suffered from the same disorder as the character.

This is because his obsessions were centred on contamination and mine are focused on violence/harm. And yet, they are the same. It is all OCD. I've heard from others in the community that it is important not to get too tied to one theme. OCD is a malevolent shapeshifter and a sufferer will often experience multiple themes in their life. But what occurred to me is that if I had grown up with a portrayal of OCD in the media that showed similar obsessions to mine – I might have been able to get treatment sooner.

In writing my book I was fuelled by this desire. I needed to add to the conversation in some small way. I couldn't stand the idea of someone going years thinking the hell of obsessive-compulsive disorder was 'just how their mind was'. Or perhaps, not being able to continue on at all. The idea that my book might reach someone out there who was struggling became everything to me.

I've always been a lurker. As a child I looked on as the others played together. I felt that acute sense of isolation and dislocation that I think all of us do. Being human can be a lonely business.

Now I find myself in a uniquely privileged position. Guts Publishing has given me the opportunity to tell my story. I've found people who are incredibly kind, who love books and aren't afraid to talk about the realities of mental illness. I realise that I've never been alone. Not really. I know that the strangest thought I've had is one someone else has had. I think that's why I really wrote the book. To one day have that email land in my inbox. Someone who found something in the book that spoke to them. I can't explain how much that would mean to me.

'Blade in the Shadow' is me sitting in the lighthouse and slowly having enough courage to turn on the beam. And hoping that someone out there does the same.

10 September 2021
Jillian Halket

Acknowledgments

To my wonderful editor Julianne Ingles. This book wouldn't exist without you. Thank you for your steadfast belief in not only the book, but in me. I don't think you know what it meant that you extended your hand and offered to share my story with the world. This journey has been mad and beautiful and I wouldn't have had any of it if it weren't for you. Thank you for being my champion. And more than that. Thank you for being an inspiration. For years when I was unwell everything was lost to me. The future didn't exist. Now there is a future. There is a book. You have helped me shape those years of trauma and hurt into something beautiful. Thank you, Julianne.

Katy, I wanted to thank you so much for everything you've done for me. I wouldn't be in this position now if it weren't for you. It can be so hard trying to get your voice heard and you lifted mine up. I will be forever grateful for that.

Thank you to my family – there would be no living without you. Whatever words I have will never be enough.

To Stuart – my brother in spirit. I've always felt you with me.

To my Grandparents. Mary and Robert. Margaret and James. I love you all. I wish we'd had more time together. I wish I could talk to you about books and films and all the strange things in life. I'll see you again soon.

To Mama. You never stopped believing. Sometimes I wonder if it was the sheer power of your intent – but we're here now. Six of swords, mad labyrinth, but we got here. I've never been truly alone in this life, because I've had you. In all those mad years – you were home. You kept me safe and healed every hurt. You held onto hope for me when I couldn't. You were my north star, guiding me through that dark time. Your silliness and laughter made me feel real joy. You showed me there was much more than the violent thoughts in my mind. That this world was filled with beauty. You made it that way. Words pale when I try to describe the love I have for you. How do you describe water to the ocean you are swimming in? You are everything to me. All that I am. I love you.

To Lydia. I've watched you with wide eyes since I was small. Taking in your kindness and humour and wanting to steal away a small piece of it for myself. If for one day you could see yourself as I do then you would know how special you are. How in a scary, dark world you light everything up. There are times I might have left the world. But I couldn't. Because of you and Mama. And I'm so grateful to have you both. Because now everything is different and I'm fighting for as much time as I can get. Your love makes life worth living.

To the best man I've ever known – Joseph. I knew as soon as I met you. I thought that kind of love was reserved for pop songs and films. But it's real. And I get to experience it with you every day we share together. You've held my hand in this life and the last. You've protected me and kept me safe and given me unconditional understanding. The past six years have felt like a dream. There was a before but it doesn't seem to mean much. Memories without you seem to have lost their colour. In bed at night I close my eyes and thank the world for bringing me here – to you. I'd do it all again – every hurt – just to meet you. It was all worth it to find you.

To Jim. You were the first person to read this book. It was like laying out my heart for someone and your kind words meant everything. You saw me. You listened. You cared. You made me feel like I was worth something – that my story was worth telling. Thank for you being the best stepdad in the world. Since you came over from Ireland with your Lord of the Rings DVDs and magick books you've been there for our family. You have always made time for me. You supported me when I was my most unwell and Mama when she was floored with her illness. You helped me understand that love is not a transaction, that I don't need to 'do' anything for someone to love me. You've no idea how much that changed things for me. Now I just feel so lucky for every weekend I get with you and Mama and the rest of the family at the Shire. Every moment is so precious. I love you.

To Craig. I was nervous when I first met you but I shouldn't have been. You are one of the most brilliant people I've ever known. I feel honoured to be your sister even though you wind me up something rotten. But isn't that, I suppose, what brothers do? Thank you for all the laughs we have shared together. Thank you for your beautiful art. Thank you for never judging me and for always making me feel safe and at home. There were many nights where I found myself in the den with you and my sister and though I wasn't well – I knew I'd be okay because I had you both. You were always the missing piece of our little family.

To the most delightful addition to all of our lives – Alexander, forever our baby Bee, and his brother and sister Poppy and David Bean. Alexander – you made our whole lives when you arrived. You are a small miracle. I'd always heard people say that, but it's true. Watching you grow is the best thing. I am so proud to be your Aunt Pea. I will buy all the Cars merchandise in the world and watch the films a thousand times over just to see you smile. Everything about you is beautiful and I can't wait to see where life takes you.

To Janice and Dave. Thank you for welcoming me into your family. Janice, I arrived in Carluke six years ago knowing no one and then I met your son and my whole world changed. You have raised the most wonderful person I've ever known. I have been blessed to be part of your family. You are both kind, gentle and admirable people. Thank you for taking care of me when I've been unwell. For all the hot baths and chocolate. I couldn't imagine my life without you in it.

To Ian. It has been wonderful to know you. It's rare to find someone who speaks with the kind of honesty you do. It makes me feel less alone. I know that whatever pain we face with mental illness there is always hope. And until then, there are chats and curries to enjoy on a Friday night as the sun sets in Carluke.

To Christopher, Crawford and Keith. My wonderful beans. I've had the pleasure of having you three in my life for fourteen years now. You made Blackwood home for me. I still remember all the adventures we had together. Though I took some strange trails through this life I've always known I could depend on you. I can't believe my luck that I found three friends as wonderful as you. I'm sorry you guys aren't in the book but I don't think the world needed twelve chapters of us talking utter nonsense. But I hope that when we are in our eighties we'll still be making silly jokes together. I love you all.

To my friends at Lesmahagow High School. You are a mad, wonderful bunch of people. I am so lucky I got to grow up with you. Maybe we should arrange a reunion in a field somewhere and build a big bonfire – for old time's sake.

To Lauren and Becca and Sooz. You've filled my life with fun, silliness and magick. At school I had to hide away anything to do with my spirituality but in your company I was free to be myself. I flourished because of you. With you it was fun to be strange, to make loud jokes in public and run around in our hippie clothes and messy hair singing loudly. I remember the teepees at Braemar and chasing the peahens. I remember weekends in the woods and beach being wild and free. Thank you for all the fun and love throughout the years. Thank you for being the most incredible and strong women.

To Uncle Alan and Adam. My best uncle and cousin. I love you both very much. Thank you Uncle Alan for CDs at Christmas and always being there to fix our washing machine when it broke. Thank you for watching documentaries with me and teaching me facts about the world. To Adam – I've watched you grow since you were a tot in your baby seat and I couldn't be more proud of the strong young man you've become. You can do anything you put your mind to.

To Aloma. Thank you for your steadfast kindness. Seven years ago you sat with me in that café at the Fort and made me believe there was something to live for. You were a friend to me in that dark time. And I have a feeling it hasn't been the first time. Thank you for everything.

To Imogen and Harry. I'm sorry your part in the book was so short because the part you played in my life certainly wasn't. Harry – I don't know if you will even read this or recognise yourself in one line. I would have put so much more in if I could.

If I didn't have your friendship in those years I wouldn't be here today. I'm still sad we stopped being in each other's lives before we could talk about how Better Call Saul was going to end.

To Miss McElhatten my Primary School teacher. Thank you for the 'Star Writer' stickers – you have no idea how much they meant to me as an anxious child. You made me believe in myself. I still have my jotters with your kind words.

To Mrs Anderton my High School English teacher. For four years you showed me the beauty and unique power of literature. I still have my copy of *Thérèse Raquin*. Thank for you making your classroom a safe haven in a chaotic time. I found so much joy there.

To Mrs Gallagher. Thank you for coming back to teach us Advanced Higher English in High School. It turns out that would be the highest qualification I would ever achieve. But don't worry – I still wrote the book. And I'm holding fast on the promise that if I ever wrote one I'd better include you. Thank you.

To the NHS, St Luke's Medical Practice, Dr. Helen, Occupational Therapy, Psychological Services and Neurology. To every medical professional that treated me with such kindness and helped me recover – I owe you my life.

To the Housing Office, Disability and Benefit workers. To See Me Scotland and SAMH. Clydesdale Community Initiative. New Lanark Heritage Site. To the Post Office ladies. Thank you.

Thank you Goddess for keeping me on the path and helping me find light in the dark.

About the Author

Jillian Halket is a writer from Blackwood, Scotland. Her debut memoir *Blade in the Shadow* delves into her obsessive compulsive disorder and explores what it is like living with violent intrusive thoughts.

She is an advocate for OCD awareness and recovery and was proud to take part in the first Activate Training for Movement for Change, a grassroots campaign by See Me Scotland. By telling her story she is determined to help in the fight against mental health stigma and discrimination.

When she is not talking about OCD, she can be found haunting the local bookshop or out in the Scottish countryside with her family and partner. She is a hippie at heart and enjoys anything to do with the occult and the written word.

About Guts Publishing

 Established in May 2019, we are an independent publisher in London. The name came from the obvious—it takes guts to publish just about anything. We are the home to the freaks and misfits of the literary world.

We like uncomfortable topics. Our tagline: Ballsy books about life. Our thinking: the book market has enough ball-less books and we're happy to shake things up a bit.

Blade in the Shadow (Oct 2021) is Jillian's debut memoir. We are delighted to bring this story to you and hope you've enjoyed reading it. Well done Jillian Halket.

Fish Town (Apr 2021) by John Gerard Fagan is our second memoir. It explores John's bittersweet departure from Glasgow and the next seven years of his life in a remote fishing village in Japan.

Euphoric Recall (Oct 2020) by Aidan Martin, is our debut memoir. The true story of a Scottish working-class lad and his and his recovery from addiction and trauma.

Sending Nudes (Jan 2021) is a collection of fiction nonfiction and poetry about the various reasons people send nudes.

Cyber Smut (Sept 2020) is a collection of fiction, nonfiction and poetry about the effects of technology on our lives, our sexuality and how we love.

Stories About Penises (Nov 2019) is a collection of fiction, nonfiction and poetry about, well, exactly what it sounds like. To quote a prominent Australian author, 'Quite possibly the best title of the year.' We think so too.

Our website: gutspublishing.com
Our email: gutspublishing@gmail.com

Thank you for reading and thank you for your support!